ANONYMOUS

Who Wrote the Epistle to the Hebrews?

Copyright © David Criswell 2013

David Criswell

ADONAI PRESS

Dallas, TX

ANONYMOUS

Who Wrote the Epistle to the Hebrews?

David Criswell

All Rights Reserved © 2013 by David Criswell

No part of the book may be reproduced or transmitted in any form or by any means, graphic, electronic, or mechanical, including photocopying, recording, taping, or by any information storage system, without the prior permission in writing from the copyright owner.

ISBN NUMBER 0-61588-733-3

Cover Design by David Criswell
Art by Rembrandt – Circa 1650s

ADONAI PRESS

Dallas, TX

Printed in the United States of America

Dedication

To my *bahin*. May she find the Lord Jesus.

"Who wrote the epistle only God knows"
– Origen.[1]

Preface

This is the second book I have written which evolved out of an appendix for my last book in the Controversies series, *Controversies in the Acts and Epistles*. By makes these as companion pieces I have saved several hundred pages of appendices and permitted myself to delve deeper into these studies than I had originally planned.

When I first began my study I had no preconceived biases, but I did have some premature prejudices in regard to the authorship of Hebrews. Since researching the issues I have since found that my favorite candidate became one of the least likely candidates and the last person I would have expected to write Hebrews became of the more promising candidates. I have still not adopted any firm stance on the issue and it is not my intent to convince anyone as to the "correct" answer. Rather I hope to present the reader will all the evidence for and against each candidate and allow him to judge for himself which is true. I hope I shall not disappoint in this regard.

David Criswell, August 2013

Table of Contents

1. Introduction 1
2. The Evidence Outlined 5
3. Suspect # 1 - Paul 33
Chart on Theory of Pauline Authorship 50
4. Suspect # 2 - Barnabas 51
Chart on Theory of Barnabas' Authorship 58
5. Suspect # 3 - Luke 59
Chart on Theory of Lukan Authorship 69
6. Suspect # 4 - Apollos 71
Chart on Theory of Apollos' Authorship 74
7. Suspect # 5 - Priscilla and Aquila 75
Chart on Theory of Priscilla and Aquila's Authorship 86
8. Suspect # 6 – Clement of Rome 87
Chart on Theory of Clemetine Authorship 97
9. Suspect # 7 - Silas 99
Chart on Theory of Silas' Authorship 102
10. Suspect # 8 - Mark 103
Chart on Theory of Markan Authorship 106
11. Other "Suspects" 107
Chart on Theory of Aristion Authorship 107
Chart on Theory of Epaphras Authorship 108
Chart on Theory of Jude Authorship 109
Chart on Theory of Petrine Authorship 115
Chart on Theory of Philip the Evangelist Authorship 117
Chart on Theory of Timothean Authorship 120
Chart on Theory of Titus Authorship 123
12. Conclusion 127
Appendix : Hebrews in the Canon 131
End Notes 139
Works Cited 147

1

Introduction

Most of the books in the Bible are not signed by the author. We know who wrote the gospel of Matthew, for example, not because the author identified himself as Matthew but based on evidence from within and without. Tradition unanimously attributes the gospel of Matthew to the apostle who bears that name. Some books, however, there is debate, but none so great as the Epistle to the Hebrews.

Despite the fact that some Bible translators are so sure that Paul wrote this epistle that they call it "the Epistle of Paul to the Hebrews," the epistle is unsigned and no historian, theologian, scholar, or church father appears to call the epistle Paul's until at least a century after it was written. In the west, where the letter was penned, Pauline authorship was actually denied until after the time of Constantine. So it is by no means clear that Paul was the author, and much evidence within the text of Hebrews lead many to believe he could not have been its author.

Other suggestions have ranged from Barnabas, whom the earliest western church fathers favored, to idle speculation like Titus or even Epaphras (Colossians 1:7; 4:12; Philippians 1:23). Some less than credible critics have even argued that the letter was sent by an impostor pretending to be Paul![2] Of course the fact that Paul's name appears nowhere in the letter, forged or not, nullifies such trivial arguments. Nevertheless, the debate over the authorship of Hebrews is a long standing one which has never been settled.

The fact that the letter is unsigned is not a problem in itself, for the apostle John did not sign most of his epistles either. Some were accustomed to formally signing their names in the salutations, while others did not. The question is, how can we identify the author if he did not? Certainly the recipients of Hebrews knew who wrote it. Indeed, whomever delivered the letter would have revealed its author, and many times scrolls were sealed with a wax seal which identified the author like a brand. No two authors would have the same seal, so like an e-mail address we can know who sent the letter without having it signed, but this still doesn't help those of us living today, for the recipients left no information as to the author. Even ancient traditions are divided. The west seemed to favor Barnabas while the east favored Paul. Other traditions have suggested Luke and even Clement (Philippians 4:3).

The purpose of this book is not to give the reader the "correct" answer, for I freely admit that I do not know who the author may have been. In fact, I wrote this book while researching the topic for *Controversies in the Acts and Epistles.* I did not know the answer then, and while I have more informed opinions, I have still not reached a conclusion. It may be that the epistle was written by someone who is not well known to Bible readers. This could, in fact, be a reason that no traditions remain as to his identity. Had, for example, Urbanus (Romans 16:9) written Hebrews then we would have no other information on him. He is mentioned only once in the Bible and not found in tradition. He was obviously a man important enough to warrant Paul's greeting, but left no legacy to be found in tradition. Does the author of Hebrews *have* to have a great legacy beyond the epistle? Many say, "yes," for he speaks as one with authority. Is this so? Together we will examine all the candidates which have been proposed through the ages and I will allow the reader to reach his own conclusions.

The first full chapter (two) will discuss the basic criteria by which we must weigh all candidates. Was the author Jewish? When did he write? Was he an associate of Timothy? These are examples of certain criteria which we can determine from the epistle of Hebrews. Once this criteria has been established then each chapter will have a similar structure for the reader's evaluation. I will lay out the evidence in favor of a particular candidate and the evidence against him. I will evaluate those evidences and render my own opinion with a small chart highlighting the strengths and weaknesses. As for the definitive answer as to whom wrote Hebrews ... I will leave the reader to determine that, if he can.

2

The Evidence Outlined

I have always likened good exegesis to good detective work. A good detective does not assume anything. Even if he suspects that someone is guilty, he treats the evidence objectively lest the defense lawyer be able to tear down his case because of sloppy or biased research. Here we have a case of an anonymous letter. As good detectives we seek to discover who wrote the epistle. However, all the eye witnesses are dead. Moreover, the crime scene has been contaminated by 2000 years of dust. How then can we determine the answer?

Detectives have several tools at their hand. The two most important are first hand eyewitnesses and forensic evidence. In the case of forensic evidence, most is no longer available. However, there are some clues within the text of the letter itself which may indicate who wrote it. Additionally, while all the first hand eyewitnesses (the author and recipients) are dead, we do have second hand witnesses. These witnesses are sometimes disallowed in court because their evidence is what is called "hear-say" evidence, or evidence heard second hand. Nevertheless, under certain circumstances "hear-say" evidence is allowed. For example, "I heard Johnny say he did it." This evidence is not sufficient by itself, but with corroborating evidence, it can be critical. Let us look at these evidences in the context of Hebrews.

The General Evidence

The best and most important evidence for the authorship of Hebrews is the Bible itself. Although Hebrews does not state who wrote it, there are evidences within which give us clues as to the author's identity. For example, most believe it is apparent that the author is a Jew. Although it is *possible* that he was not, the heavy emphasis upon Jewish rituals, practices, and beliefs make it extremely unlikely that a gentile would be one to teach Jews about Judaism. Such internal evidences will be dealt with primarily in each chapter, but here it is my purpose to lay out the general evidence by which we can determine criteria which may help pinpoint our "suspect's" identity.

Other evidences may render clues as well. Tradition is, of course, one point of emphasis, but of no less importance is the date of the epistle, its content, and even to whom the epistle was written. All these give us hints that will play an important role in determining who wrote Hebrews. Nonetheless, I will not make any firm conclusions at this stage. Rather the purpose here is to familiarize the reader with the evidences which will factor into our discussions of various candidates. The date of the epistle, for example, proves nothing in its self, but when we examine the candidates we must take a fresh look at the dates to see whether or not a particular candidate was in a position to have written such an epistle as such a date and time.

The Date of the Epistle

Like the name of its author, the date at which it was written does not appear within the epistle to the Hebrews. However, there are many indications as to the date of the epistle from within and without. We cannot know the exact date, but we can establish a time frame in which it was written. This time frame can be helpful, and even critical, in determining which candidates, or "suspects" as per my analogy, could have written the epistle.

Based on internal Biblical evidence (as will be discussed below) most agree that the earliest possible date would be sometime in the fifties. At the latest Hebrews cannot far pre-date 1 Clement, written around 95 A.D., for Clement appear to quote from Hebrews. Thus, the wide range for Hebrew's authorship is between circa 55 and 90 A.D. A closer examination of the text reveals that we can narrow its date of composition much further.

The Second Generation

First, most believe that Hebrews is written to second generation Christians. According to Hebrews 2:3 the author of Hebrews aligns himself with his readers as those who had "heard" the gospel second hand from the original followers of Christ. This makes both the readers and author second generation believers, although there is no indication that any great time had elapsed. However, the allusion to "former days" in 10:32 is evidence that the days of Jesus and their original conversion were many years in the past. If the author is urging them to remember their "former days" and encouraging them not to abandon their zeal in the coming days of trials and tribulation, then we may logically conclude that at least a decade or two had passed.

This is further supported by 5:12 which implies that some time had passed since their conversion, for they are being chastised for not having matured in the faith. However, the strongest indication that the readers were removed from Jesus by several decades appears in 13:7 where the author asked them to "remember those who led you." If they had to "remember" those who had "led" (past tense) them, then it is obvious that those leaders have either moved on, or more likely, passed on.

We cannot establish a date based upon this evidence, but we can rule out Hebrews being one of the earlier epistles. Reasonably, it cannot be dated before the late fifties at the *earliest*.

The Temple Destruction

Second, despite a plethora of analogies and references to the Tabernacle, there is not a single mention of the destruction of the Temple which is one of the most significant events in Jewish history. To this very day Jews commemorate *Tisha B'Av* (the ninth day of the month of Av). The reasons are many and not without Biblical importance. Here is why. The date of the Temple's destruction was the ninth of Av (roughly corresponding to late July–early August) in 70 A.D. The first Temple was also destroyed on the *same day* in 587 B.C.[3] Additionally, tradition holds that the ninth of Av is also when the spies reported to Moses that they could not take the land of Canaan for fear of the giants (Numbers 13), thus resulting in the original generation being condemned to wander the desert for forty years.

Thus *Tisha B'Av* has been seen as a day of judgment assigned by God. The destruction of the Temple, prophesied by Jesus in Matthew 24:2 (cf. Mark 13:2; Luke 19:44, 21:6), is thus one of the most significant events in the history of Judaism. No student of Judaism can deny this. It would therefore be extremely odd that the author of Hebrews never even alludes to this prophetic event[4] if it had already happened. Therefore, most agree that Hebrews was written sometime before 70 A.D. when the Temple was still standing.

Francesco Hayez – The Destruction of the Temple of Jerusalem – 1867

Nonetheless, there are some who contest this. They argue that this is an argument from silence and that the book of Hebrews constantly refers to the Tabernacle, but not the Temple.[5] This, they say, implies that the Temple did not exist.[6] While at first these arguments may sound solid, a closer examination reveals their weakness.

In regard to the first criticism, it should be noted that while arguments from silence are rarely condemning, they can be. A historian, for example, who writes a history of the Jews but ignores the Holocaust would either be completely ignorant or we would have to conclude that he wrote *before* the Holocaust. Those are the only two options available. The same can be said for the Temple destruction, commemorated to this day by Jews world wide.

The second criticism sounds even more strong until we realize that the author of Hebrews is quoting from the *Torah* or *Pentateuch*. Since the *Torah* was written before the Temple had been built, it could *only* refer to the Tabernacle. Citation from the *Torah* only prove that the *Torah* was written before the Temple was build, not that the book of Hebrews was written after its destruction.

Logically, the strong Levitical nature of Hebrews and its discussion of the Tabernacle (the early portable version of the later Temple) rituals demonstrates that the author would not have ignored one of Israel's most historically, and prophetically, important events had it already occurred. This is thus strong evidence held by almost all serious Bible scholars that Hebrews was written before 70 A.D.

Persecution

Third, Hebrews appears to have been written during a time of persecution. Verses 10:32-36 urges the recipients to remain steadfast while 12:4 makes it clear that they may well have to shed their blood. The phrase "not yet" implies that such is a distinct possibility. Now while persecutions were sporadic throughout the empire from pagan and Jews alike, there were two main periods of persecution in the first half century after Christ. The early church was persecuted under the priesthood (cf. Acts 7, 12:2, etc.). This was the first persecution which may or may not have been to what the author alludes in Hebrews 10:32-33. The second period of persecution came under Nero, beginning in 64 A.D. and co-incided with the Great Revolt in Israel which began in 66 A.D. As a result, Christians were persecuted as traitors by Jewish rebels, as described by Josephus and elsewhere.[7] Since verses 2:3, 5:12, and 13:7 effectively rule out the early persecutions of Acts, and since the author appears to be alluding to a more systematic persecution than the sporadic ones that took place earlier, it follows that the epistle must have been written after these later persecutions began, no earlier than 65 or 66 A.D.

Timothy

Fourth, Hebrews 13:23 states that "our brother Timothy has been released." Timothy, of course, was imprisoned by Nero during the infamous persecutions in which Peter and Paul met their martyrdom. Although we do not know the exact circumstances of Timothy's imprisonment and release, it is obvious that after 65 A.D. Nero was not releasing Christian prisoners. However, Timothy's imprisonment *appears* to co-incide with Paul's second imprisonment (Philemon 1:1) from which he would not escape. Paul was beheaded by Nero sometime between 65 and 68 A.D.[8] Consequently, it appears most likely that Timothy was not released from prison until after Nero's death in 68 A.D., miraculously escaping death. This would then fix the date for Hebrews sometime after 68 A.D.

The Great Revolt

To the usual arguments, I add a fifth. Hebrews 10:29-31 offers a strong indication that the Great Revolt, and perhaps even the siege of Jerusalem, had already begun.

> "How much severer punishment do you think he will deserve who has trampled under foot the Son of God, and has regarded as unclean the blood of the covenant by which he was sanctified, and has insulted the Spirit of grace? For we know Him who said, 'Vengeance is mine, I will repay.' And again, 'The LORD will judge His people.' It is a terrifying thing to fall into the hands of the living God" (10:29-31).

Such a sober warning of coming judgment fits well against the backdrop and context of the letter. Those Jews who followed Christ had been rejected as heretics and were cast out. Earlier persecutions (alluded to in 10:32) had come largely from Jewish priests and their followers. Now the Roman persecutions had begun against Christians in the west, and against Israel in the east.

Logically, the warnings and discussion of Levitical practices written to a Jewish audience make the most sense against the backdrop of this war which had begun in 66 A.D. This is further evidence that Hebrews should be dated after the rebellion began.

Conclusion

Based on the five evidences it is apparent that Hebrews had to have been written after 66 A.D. and before 70 A.D. Given Timothy's release from prison and the imminent threats alluded to in 10:29-36, we may further narrow the date of Hebrew's writing to sometime between 68 and 69 A.D.

Tradition
Tradition falls into the category of "hear-say." By itself it is almost useless, but the earlier the tradition, the better. It is like gossip around a table. The first person to hear the story is closest to the truth, but by the time the story has been passed around to the end of the table there is often little semblance left of the truth. Tradition therefore plays a role, but only a small one.

Style and Vocabulary
Almost every advocate claims that the style and vocabulary of Hebrews matches whomever he believes wrote Hebrews. Advocates of Paul say it is Paul's style while advocates of Luke argue it is his style and others argue that it is the style of Clement of Rome or others. I will discuss such arguments in each chapter, but not in depth for it is my firm belief that such arguments are drastically overrated, and I shall justify this belief here.

My father used to tell me two "old west Texas sayings," or so he claimed they were. First, he said, "figures don't lie, but liars can sure figure!" The second I am pretty sure did not really originate from west Texas, but is relevant nonetheless. "Son," he said, "there are three kinds of lies in this world. Lies. Damn lies. And statistics." During the Obama administration, Obama touted a 7.6% unemployment rate (he "inherited" 7.5%). Conversely a recent Associate Press poll said that 80% of Americans struggle with poverty and joblessness (yes, 80%).[9] Somewhere between these two extremes lies the truth. The 7.6% number ignores welfare recipients and those not on "unemployment compensation." The 80% counts all those who have not had full time jobs for a year or more. Each views poverty differently and count the numbers differently. The same is true with arguments for "style" and "vocabulary." Let me give some startling statistics of my own.

According to one Biblical research analysis "37% of vocabulary in 2 Maccabees recurs in Acts; 35% of vocabulary in 2 Maccabees recurs in Luke; 30% of vocabulary in 2 Maccabees recurs in Matthew; 44% of vocabulary in 3 Maccabees recurs in Acts; 43% of vocabulary in 3 Maccabees recurs in Luke; and 34% of vocabulary in 3 Maccabees recurs in Matthew."[10] Additionally, Hebrews has 22% with in common with 2 Maccabees and 28% with 3 Maccabees![11] Considering that Maccabees was written hundreds of years earlier, it is probably safe to say that they were not written by the same person. Nevertheless, one scholar touts the fact that there are 34% similarities between nouns used in Luke and Hebrews[12] and 35% of the verbs used in Luke are found in Hebrews.[13] He then adds various numbers together to claim that 67% of vocabulary in Luke and Acts (together) is also found in Hebrews.[14]

My response to such numbers is that 99% of the vocabulary found in this book are also to be found in Webster's Dictionary, but only 2% of the words found in it are found in this book! Did I write

Webster's dictionary? Now before the reader dismisses my comments are pure sarcasm (even though they are), I do not completely dismiss arguments from style and vocabulary, but I do find them subjective and misleading. The vocabulary and style found in my history books differ dramatically from my theological works which in turn differ drastically from my fiction works. Those who have read all the thousands of pages I have written may be able to recognize my style even across genre, but consider that the largest book in the Bible is smaller than most books written today. Can we really positively identify an author based on a limited comparison of style and vocabulary? Obviously not. It is, however, one factor to be considered.

Some have called Hebrews a "systematic" theology,[15] but it has also been said that it is a "style is unlike that of any other New Testament document."[16] This is true. Consequently, style arguments have their limits. As a result I will touch upon style arguments in each chapter when relevant, but I will not enter into lengthy debates based on suspect opinions and statistics. Let the reader judge for himself how much merit those arguments may or may not have.

Recipients
The question of the recipients of the letter has two aspects. One is their ethnicity and the other is the city or region in which they lived. Both could possibly help to shed light upon the author.

The title, "to the Hebrews," would seem to indicate the answer to the first aspect, but like the author, the title is not actually found in the text of the epistle itself. Consequently, there are actually three different theories upon the generic make-up of the recipients; that they were Jews; that they were gentiles; or that they were a mixture.

The argument that the recipients were gentiles is obviously the least popular since the title universally bestowed upon the epistle suggest otherwise. Nevertheless, some have argued that just as there were Jews in Rome when Paul wrote the book of Romans, so also the appearance of Jews in Hebrews does not negate a predominantly gentile audience.[17] They argue that the explanation of Jewish law would not have been necessary if the author was writing to Jews. However, the author is not so much explaining Jewish law, as if the readers did not know it, but demonstrating how Jesus is the ultimate fulfillment of the law. If you wanted to present the gospel to your Hindu friend, which book would you use; Romans or Hebrews? The answer to this invalidates the theory that the recipients were gentile in any great number.

Obviously most believe that Jews were dominant, if not exclusive, make-up of the readers, but some have argued that they were specifically priests. Ceslas Spicq believed that the Jews were priests formerly from the Qumran community.[18] On the other hand J.V. Brown argued that they were actually the Jewish priests of Acts 6:7.[19] He presented twelve evidences to support this theory.[20]

1) Based on Hebrews 2:3 he argued that they must have been converted by apostles (cf. Acts 6:7; Hebrew 5:12; 10:32). This first point seems a sound thesis.

2) He argues that they would have known Roman Jews at Pentecost based on Acts 2:10. This is relevant since most believe Hebrews was written from Rome (see notes below). However, it is somewhat of a thin argument, for there were Jews from all over the empire, and the fact that they may have known some Roman Jews makes for a tenuous connection with Hebrews 13:24.

3) He argues that the "signs and wonders and various miracles" of Hebrews 2:4 are allusions to Acts 6:8 and Stephen's miracles. Nevertheless, this too is tenuous for Stephen was not the only one who performed such miracles and if they were converts of the apostles, as postulated in the first point, then they could certainly have seem the apostles' miracles.

4) He argues that Hebrews 5:12 shows that they were teachers, which was the job of priests. However, 5:12 actually says they *should* be teachers by now, but were not qualified. This is not a valid argument.

5) He attempts to link "another priest arises" in Hebrews 7:15 with Acts 20:17-18, 28, but this argument seems particularly weak. The new priest of Hebrews is Christ! The elders and priests of Acts 20 are mere men, some of whom are heretics (v. 30)!

6) He points out that they were familiar with the temple and thus must have visited it often. This is a stronger argument although not entirely convincing. They were certainly familiar with the *Torah* from which Hebrews quoted, and this could have been sufficient.

7) He suggests that Hebrews 13:10 implies a certain temptation to follow Jewish laws in regard to temple food. Certainly this shows that they were Jewish, if not priests.

8) He argues that Hebrews 10:18 would have been directly relevant to priests, since sacrifices was one of their primary jobs. This is actually one of the strongest points Brown makes, for the author is saying that the sacrifices of

the Temple are no longer necessary in this dispensation. Such a remark would have profound impact upon priests in a time when Jerusalem was nearing, if not already under, siege.

9) He argues that the Melchizedek model was used to avoid criticism of Levites, but this argument seems forced. The order of Melchizedek should be take for what the author presents it as; a type of the true priesthood.

10) He argues that Hebrews 6:6 and 10:29 "is better understood against the backdrop of readers who had taken part in the death of Jesus."[21] In regard to Hebrews 10:29 I would agree that there is a strong allusion to those who actually took part in Christ's crucifixion, but the allusion in 6:6 is probably relevant to any apostate.

11) He further argues that the comments about being "rich" (Hebrews 13:12) reflect the Sadducees who he regards as the rich priestly caste. This, however, is a suspect argument.

12) Finally, he notes that the ancient title "to the Hebrews" "suggest a homogeneous group."[22] The only place where Jews would be in dominance of the church is Israel.

As the reader can see, the twelve points have good and bad arguments. I personally consider half of the arguments valid and half invalid. The strongest points suggest that if the church members were converts of the apostles who witnesses miracles and were concerned with the priesthood and sacrifices, then they must have been converted in Israel. Certainly they were Jewish, and that there were priestly converts among them may also be true.

The strongest evidence may be if the date for the epistle of Hebrews, which I offered above, is correct. If so then it is more than likely that Christian priests were driven out of Jerusalem shortly before the Roman siege. This would explain their concerns about ritual sacrifices, which would soon be halted. This may also be hinted at by Josephus who even considered the siege of Jerusalem to be God's punishment for the murder of James the Just![23] Thus, he states that the siege began shortly after the apostle's martyrdom in Jerusalem. During this time the rebel leaders would have expelled Christians from Jerusalem, if they had not already been expelled after James's death. This then begs the question. Were the recipients actually in Jerusalem at the time Hebrews was written? If they had been driven out of Jerusalem, then where were they? Upon this there is no agreement. No fewer than nine different locations have been suggested over the years.

Jerusalem

The belief that Hebrews was written to Jews in Jerusalem has been a long standing view of many scholars. The three primary evidences are 1) the fact that the audience appears to have been predominantly Jewish. 2) The belief that Hebrews 13:12 indicates readers familiarity with Jewish city layout.[24] 3) The belief that Hebrews 10:32-34 refers to Jewish persecution[25] which would not have occurred outside of Palestine.

Now it has been noted that "since the readers were second generation Christians (2:3), it is hard to see how the writer could, with propriety, praise them for their stead-fastness under persecutions which they did not even endure,"[26] but this is not entirely accurate. Many had not seen Christ themselves, but this is not proof that they did not endure persecutions in Israel. Too often historians pretend like persecutions took place solely at specific times and places, and it is true that the most severe persecutions were restricted to government persecutions such as that of Nero, but persecutions took place sporadically throughout history; particularly in the early days of Christianity in and around Jerusalem. This is the reason that many Christians (including second generation Christians) fled Jerusalem and moved to Phoenicia, Cyprus, and Antioch (Acts 11:19).

Arguments against Jerusalem include the fact that Hebrews was apparently written in Greek, not Hebrew[27] (see argument below). If this is so, then it would be odd to expect that someone would write a Greek letter to Jewish recipients in Jerusalem. This argument, if true, has some merit, but the application of it is suspect. Might the epistle have been written by someone who did not know Hebrew? Can we say for sure that it was not translated into Greek? This argument must be viewed with caution.

A weak argument is by Alford who said, "If the epistle were addressed to the church at Jerusalem, it seems strange that no allusion should be made in it to the fact that the Lord Himself had lived and taught among them in the flesh, had before their eyes suffered death on the cross, had found among them the first witnesses and His resurrection and Ascension."[28] Additionally, F.W. Farrar argued along these same lines that "His references to the Tabernacle rather than to the Temple seem to make it improbable that he had ever been at Jerusalem,"[29] but these type of arguments are feeble. We cannot say that someone *should*, *might*, or *ought* to have said unless it is of significance and importance to the discussion. Moreover, the author was quoting the Pentateuch so we would not expect him to discuss the Temple specifically, as opposed to the Tabernacle. These sort of arguments should be used with caution. Also note that some believe that Hebrews 13:12 does make reference to Jerusalem.[30]

The strongest argument against Jerusalem is based on my date for the composition of Hebrews. If it was written in 68 or 69 A.D. then Hebrews 10:29-31 is probably an allusion to the Great Revolt and/or the siege of Jerusalem. If this is true then it is impossible that Jewish Christians were still living in the city. They would have been driven out by the rebels after the martyrdom of James the Just, described in Josephus.[31]

Another Israeli City

If the recipients had left, or been driven out, of Jerusalem, then we might ponder to where they had fled. Antioch is one of the most popular choices. In the book of Acts it is listed as the relocated center of the apostles' ministry (cf. Acts 11, 14-15). However, Theodore Zahn argues that Antioch was already predominantly gentile by the time of Hebrews writing, based on Acts 15:1, 23 and Galatians 2:11-14,[32] but Acts hardly proves that Antioch was "predominantly" gentile. It only says that some were teaching gentile converts to be circumcised. This is the circumcision debate and says *nothing* of the percentage of gentiles in Antioch.

Another suggestion has been Caesarea, but there seems little evidence to promote one city over another. It is likely that the Christians of Jerusalem did relocate to another city. This relocation did not cease persecution, however, as the author of Hebrews warned that they may soon face death (12:4).

Ephesus
Ephesus was a major city for Christians. Paul and John both ministered there and it was one of the major churches of Asia Minor. Some have tried to make Ephesus the location of the city for various reasons; sometimes agenda driven reasons.[33] One even argues that the "theater" (θεατρον) of Acts 19:29, 31 and the "spectacle" (θεατριζομενοι) in Hebrews 10:33 indicate that are one and same.[34] Despite the rather speculative arguments made to support this thesis, there is no evidence to support a majority Jewish population. In fact, Ruth Hoppin, who argues fervently for Ephesus herself states that Ephesus had "the largest ratio of converts to total population" and "many gentile converts."[35] She thus negates her own arguments for if Hebrews was indeed written to Hebrews, then there should not be a greater gentile population than Hebrew population. Ephesus cannot realistically be the location of the city to which Hebrews was written.

Cyprus
Another argument is made for Cyprus, one of the cities mentioned in Acts 11:19. Nonetheless, aside from this passage there is no particular evidence to support it. It is usually presented solely by those who believe that Barnabas, who was from Cyprus, was the author of Hebrews, even though there is no reason that Barnabas could not have easily written to any number of other cities.

Alexandria, Egypt

Among the more serious non-Israel contenders is Alexandria, Egypt. Alexandria was the most important church in Africa. Believed to have been founded by Mark, it was one of the largest cities in the ancient world, with around 700,000 people.[36]

Another clue might be found in the Muratorian Canon; an ancient list of New Testament books that omits the book of Hebrews but includes an epistle to the Alexandrians, which some believe is the same as Hebrews.[37] This epistle to the Alexandrians is either no longer in existence, or is an alternate name for Hebrews.

Arguments for Alexandria include the following:[38]

1) Greek was language of Alexandria and would explain why Greek, rather than Hebrew, was used in a letter to Jews.

2) It would also explain the use of Greek *Septuagint* rather than the Hebrew *Torah*.

3) The "author brought out of the Old Testament by his quotations from the LXX things which are not seen in the Hebrew text."[39]

4) Types and allegories, such as are found in Hebrews, were presumed to be popular in Alexandria.

5) The writer allegedly quotes 2 Maccabees (11:35-37) which was written in Alexandria.

6) There is the assumption that Hebrews 10:32-34 was a reference to the slaughter of Jews in Alexandria under Caligula.[40]

7) There is the argument that discussions of Tabernacle rituals differs from Jerusalem and this is

because it actually refers to a famous Alexandrian temple (cf. 7:27; 9:1).[41]

While these arguments sound substantial at first, there are severe problems with several of these points. The argument that types and allegories were popular in Alexandria is rather anachronistic and misleading. Certainly Clement of Alexandria and Origen were highly allegorical, but they lived long after Hebrews written. Moreover, Philo's influence is overstated, for the allegory of Hebrews is different from that found the aforementioned. The allegory of Origen, for example, denied the historicity of many Biblical events, whereas the author of Hebrews clearly accepted the historicity of all the events in the Bible, and even some of the non-Biblical stories, such as that of Enoch.

Another problem is that the attempt to connect Hebrews 10:32-34 with the events in Alexandria under Caligula is suspect to say the least. So also is the alleged quotation from Maccabees. Maccabees is based on actual historical events of great significance to the Jewish people. It seems a stretch to argue that this is a quote from Maccabees or that it is cited to appeal to Alexandrians.

The final argument in regard to the temple is not only highly speculative, but caters to false allegations that Hebrews "errs" in regard to certain Jewish rituals (see my *Controversies in Acts and the Epistles*). There is no reason to believe that the Alexandrian temple plays even the slightest role in Hebrews as the entire quotations are from the Bible itself!

Another problem with Alexandria is the predominant population of gentiles. The context of Hebrews is not only heavily Jewish, but the backdrop appears to be coming persecutions and probably the War of the Jews. The War of the Jews did not effect Alexandria at all, and the persecutions of Nero, although were by no means confined to Rome as some claim,[42] were scarcely felt in Alexandria where the emperor's influence dwindled. The civil war which erupted to overthrow Nero broke the power he had over Gaul, Germania, and probably most of northern Africa as well. Therefore, despite its promise, the church of Alexandria is most probably not the ones to whom Hebrews was written.

Rome
Another popular view is that Rome, or more generically Italy, was not the city *from* which the author was writing, as Hebrews 13:24 might imply, but that it was the city *to* which he was writing. The crux of the argument revolves around the meaning of "they of Italy." Hebrews 13:24 says "they of Italy greet you." Some argue that "they of Italy" should be interpreted to mean "that which are borne away, or separated."[43] In other words, it is argued that the Greek *ablative* case infers that "they of Italy" were away from Italy and sending greetings back home.[44]

In order to further bolster their case, they note that "from Italy" in Acts 18:2, when Aquila had been expelled from Rome, is also in the ablative case.[45] Despite the seeming strength, this is actually a very weak argument. It may sound convincing to those not versed in Greek, but it is in reality grasping at straws. To start with it is obvious that "they of Italy" were separated from the readers regardless of where the readers were located! Second, my college Greek text explains that there are two types of genitives (the possessive form); descriptive and separative.[46] In other words, if I say "of Italy" it can either mean something that *belongs to* Italy or someone *from* Italy. One is a description, such as "John's book" (the book *of* John), whereas the other is not, such as "he read it *from* the book." As A.T. Roberston stated, "the preposition does not determine whether the persons were still in Italy or are outside of Italy."[47]

Other claims include the idea that the mention of Italy proves that he was well known in Rome,[48] although this would also make sense if the letter was written from Rome, rather than to Rome!

Finally, they argue that these people "of Italy" are the same as those expelled by Claudius in Acts 18:2, but this cannot be so for it is a historical fact that following Claudius' death the Jews were allowed to return to their homes in 54 A.D.[49] This would have been well over a decade before Hebrews was even written. It is thus wild speculation to suggest that these people were not living in Rome at the time of the letter.

The best argument against Italy being the destination of the letter, rather than its source, is the fact that the author informs the readers that Timothy has been released from prison (13:23). Since Timothy was imprisoned in Rome it makes sense that the one in the know would be the one *in* Rome. The recipients were apparently not aware because they were not in Rome.

A final argument against Rome being the destination city, although not the best, is the postscript found in the King James Bible. It reads, "written to the Hebrews from Italy, by Timothy" (13:25). This postscript is found in various slightly differing forms in the Codex Sinaiticus (א), Alexandrinus (A), and Ephraemi (C) as well as the Majority text (𝔐) passed down through the church. It is, however, missing from most all other ancient manuscripts including the most ancient Papyrus 46 ($\mathfrak{P}^{46}$). Consequently, the postscript is omitted from all modern translations including the New King James. Nevertheless, its antiquity supports the fact that the Roman church believed the letter to have been sent *from* Italy, and not *to* Italy. This would seem to be the most natural reading of the text, as well as the context, for the recipients were clearly predominantly Jewish. Although Rome did have a large percentage of Jews (as much as 10%), we would be hard stretched to claim that the congregation of Rome was predominately Jewish in character.

Other Suggestions

Other cities have been suggested as well. Galatia is mentioned in Acts 11:19. Others have believed that Thessolonica was the city in question. These other suggestions, however, have little evidence and are mere speculations.

It seems then that the best suggestion is that Hebrews was written to Jews who had been driven out of Jerusalem shortly before the siege of the city by Roman forces. We cannot say what city they lived in, but it is clear that they were not safe from persecution which still appeared imminent. Nonetheless, it is likely that they were still residing somewhere in Israel.

The Language of Hebrews
A final intriguing question remains. If the epistle was written to a Jewish community then why would it be written in Greek rather than Hebrew? The usual answer is that it was translated into Greek by either Luke or Clement of Rome.[50] Nonetheless, some have argued that Hebrews could in no way be a translation from Hebrew. They argue that there are too many *paranomosias* (Greek word plays) and similar stylistic Greek which could not have come from Hebrew or Aramaic.[51] I will not debate this here, but reserve debate for those chapters where the translation issue become relevant. My purpose here is for the reader to be aware that the author either 1) could not read and write Hebrew or 2) probably did not translate Hebrews himself. Which of these opinions we take may yield clues as to the author's identity.

Evidences Summarized

What can we deduce about the author of Hebrews from these facts? Commentators differ, but of the following we can at least be fairly certain:

1. The Author Was Jewish
This generally agreed upon by most. Although the Greek may hint at a gentile author, the text of the epistle is strongly Hebrew, and made with authority. It is hard to believe that a gentile could, or

would, speak with authority on matters of the Jewish religion, especially if the recipients were priests and/or predominantly Jews. Moreover, Hebrews 2:16 strongly indicates a Jewish author.[52]

2. The Author Wrote shortly before the Temple Fell

Although there is debate as the exact date of the epistle, it seems highly likely that the epistle was written during the Great Revolt and either during or immediately after the Neronian persecutions. My own proposed date is between 68 and 69 A.D. when Jerusalem was under siege and the Christians had been evicted from the city by rebels. This is relevant not only for context, but for the simple reason that the author must then have been alive at that time and, as we shall see, many of the candidates were not.

3. The Author Was Fluent in Greek

Although some believe that Hebrews is a translation from Hebrew, most believe that the Greek is the original. One scholars declares that the author must have had a "double background" in both Greek and Jewish.[53] Additionally, many argue that the author was a "Hellenist" well versed in both the Jewish philosopher Philo and Alexandrian thought in general.[54] On this, I do not fully agree. It is true that the author quoted entirely from the *Septuagint* translation but it is a leap to assume that he was a Hellenist, especially considering the overwhelming emphasis upon Jewish rituals. Hellenists compromised Jewish customs with Greek customs; something the author does not appear to endorse. We can, however, say that the author was well versed in Greek. On that most all agree.

4. The Author Never Met Jesus

With few exceptions, most agree that Hebrews 2:3 indicates that the author never met Jesus and that he was a second generation Christian converted after the resurrection and ascension. If true, this means he could not have been an apostle, even though he spoke as one with authority. He was, therefore, an authoritative leader of the early church, but not a first generation apostle.

5. The Author Was Well Educated and Eloquent

The eloquence and education of the author is apparent to all. He was a learned man who was able to communicate himself in an articulate and graceful way.

6. The Author Was An Associate of Timothy

He knew Timothy and was an associate of him (13:23). Most believe that this makes the author a part of Paul's inner circle, if not Paul himself. Similarities to "Pauline theology" have also reinforced this view.

7. The Author Had Authority Among the Jews

Whomever wrote Hebrews was recognized as one with authority among its recipients. This fact cannot be ignored.

Even if we grant for error in one of these, we would still say that for any candidate to be taken seriously as the author of Hebrews he would have to pass at least six of these seven basic criteria. Moreover, I have omitted debatable criteria such as the fact that the author was almost certainly in Rome when the epistle was written. All these factors must be taken into consideration before we can make a judgment. Unfortunately, the reader will see that none of the candidates can *fully* satisfy all seven criteria, let alone those additional criteria, such as residence in Rome, which are required. We must, therefore, examine each candidate, or "suspect" as per my police analogy, thoroughly. I will leave to the reader to reach his own conclusions.

3

Suspect # 1 – Paul

Some Bibles contain the title "The Epistle of Paul to the Hebrews," so we might assume that it is a foregone conclusion that Paul wrote the epistle, save the fact that the title is *not* found in the epistle (Scripture) but was added by translators. In fact, "in the western church no single writer of the first, second, or even third century attributed it to St. Paul."[55] The idea that Paul was the author does appear in the eastern church relatively early but was rejected by the western church, and Rome, until the late fourth century.

Now tradition does have its place, but the test of trust lies in the text of the epistle and in the evidences which surround it. Why would Paul write anonymously since he clearly identified himself in every other letter he wrote? Does the letter bear the "stamp" of Paul's other epistles? Does Paul fit the criteria required for the author? All of these must be examined before we can reach a conclusion either positive or negative.

The Tradition of Paul
It is debated as to exactly when Pauline authorship was first proposed. Clement of Alexandria is sometimes considered the first. He was taught under the famed Pantaenus in the end of the second century and because bishop of Alexandria in the early third century. Unfortunately, we do not have copies of his

writings about Hebrews. We only have the testimony of the fourth century historian Eusebius who records that Clement taught that Paul wrote Hebrews, but that it was translated into Greek by Luke.[56]

It thus appears that the eastern Church, which included Egypt, at least heard of the Pauline theory as early as the late second or early third century. Support in the eastern church includes ancient Syriac texts that contain Paul's name,[57] although the earlier Peshitta Syriac does not contain Paul's name and places Hebrews, like our Bibles, after the Pauline epistles.[58]

Vasily Ivanovich Surikov – Apostle Paul Before King Agrippa – 1875

Nevertheless, Pauline authorship was not supported in the western church until late fourth century.[59] In fact, "it was at Rome that the Pauline authorship was most consistently denied and for the longest period."[60] The Muratorian Canon, Irenaeus, Gaius of Rome, and Tertullian all rejected Pauline authorship.[61]

Thus it was not until the late fourth century that the church began to accept Pauline authorship. In the east Severian of Gabala went so far as to call "heretics" those who deny Paul's authorship,[62] although he subscribed to the belief that it was translated into Greek by either Luke or Clement of Rome.[63] The west still disputed the book, with Origen claiming that only God knows who wrote Hebrews. Indeed, it was not until the Council of Trent in the sixteenth century that Pauline authorship was officially recognized by the Catholic church.[64]

Theories on Anonymous Authorship
Every recognized epistle of Paul begins with his name in the first verse addressing the body to whom he was writing, and many also end with a postscript bearing his name. If Hebrews was written by Paul, it is the only letter which he wrote anonymously. The logical question is, "why?"

Theodore of Mapsuestia may have been one of the first to argue that Paul wrote anonymously to Jews on account of the Jews' hatred of him.[65] Thomas Aquinas also suggested that he wrote anonymously because "his name was odious to the Jews"[66] and also because he did not want to usurp the apostolate to the Jews.[67]

To the first argument, it may be easily answered, as J. Dwight Pentecost said, that since Paul "was addressing believers ... there would be no reason for anonymity."[68] The idea that Paul would write anonymously out of fear of the Jews is inherently weak. He wrote to *Christians*. Their Jewish heritage is irrelevant to the anonymity argument. Paul neither feared the Jews, nor hid from them. In fact, "according to Paul's custom, he went to" the Jews first, and only then went to the gentiles (cf. Romans 1:16, 2:9-10). There is no indication that Paul would have withheld his name from an epistle on account of Jews.

The second argument by Thomas Aquinas is also weak. To say that he wrote anonymously because he did not want to usurp the "apostolate" of the Jews[69] fails the test of logic. It is true that Paul considered himself an "apostle of gentiles" (Romans 11:13. cf. 1 Timothy 2:7), but even if we concluded from this that he would not preach unto the Jews (which is contradicted by his tradition of visiting Jews *first*) we cannot say that refusing to sign his name to a letter he wrote would somehow negate any usurpation. If it were a usurpation for Paul to have written to the Jews, then he *was* usurping the apostolate regardless of whether he signed the letter or not. Moreover, while we do not know who wrote the letter, the recipients *did*.

It would seem then that no advocate for Paul has found sufficient grounds for explaining the omission of his name. If Paul did write the epistle to the Hebrews, then he would have to have had a good reason for deliberately omitting his name, and because all his other epistles bear his name (many twice), we cannot simply dismiss the omission lightly as we might if another author, not accustomed to signing his name, had done so.

"Style" and Vocabulary
I have already discussed my distaste for placing too heavy an emphasis upon "style" and vocabulary. The topics which are addressed in Hebrews are not exclusive to Hebrews but found in many of Paul's epistles (see below) so it is natural that we would expect a fair amount of vocabulary common to both.

"Style" is the more subjective of the two and different authors will argue countless examples of similarities in styles or differences in styles. One theologian will argue that they were written by the same author, while another will argue that they could not have been written by the same person. Merrill Unger, for example, declares that "the style and are vocabulary not particularly Pauline,"[70] whereas another argues that closing passage of Hebrews, "grace be with you all" (13:25), is distinctly Pauline.[71] Indeed, some variant of this appears in Romans 16:24, 1 Corinthians 16:23, 2 Corinthians 13:14, Colossians 4:18, 1 Thessalonians 5:28, 2 Thessalonians 3:18, 1 Timothy 6:21, 1 Timothy 4:22, and Titus 3:15. However, when we examine the argument more closely it becomes circumstantial evidence *at best*. In Revelation, John ends his letter with almost the exact same words, saying, "the grace of the Lord Jesus be with all" (22:21). This is not unusual. In my countless e-mails to friends, many sign their e-mails with a phrase similar to "in Jesus name" or "in Him." It is clear that the salutations of Hebrews are similar to both Paul and John's in Revelation, but since we have already established that the author was an associate of Timothy and likely of Paul as well, the argument disintegrates, for they would all have probably shared the same customary greetings and salutations.

The greater problem for Pauline advocates on this front is the Greek of Hebrews. Paul prided himself on his knowledge of the *Torah* and of Hebrew. However, the Greek of Hebrews includes exclusively quotations from the *Septuagint*, the famed Greek translation of the Bible. Although Paul did sometimes quote from the *Septuagint* he often translated directly from Hebrew, for he was fluent in both Greek and Hebrew.

As aforementioned, many believe it likely that Hebrews was written exclusively in Greek, not Hebrew. This would be odd indeed if the author was fluent in Hebrew, for the recipients were almost certainly Jews. Why write in Greek an epistle with numerous quotations from the *Pentateuch* for Jews whose primary language (and the language of the *Pentateuch*) is Hebrew? Only two answers have been offered.

One answer is that Hebrews was actually written to gentiles rather than Jews as often presumed. However, I have previously addressed this issue in chapter two. It is apparent that the recipients were predominantly, if not exclusively, Jews and not gentiles.

The second answer is better as it relies upon the ancient tradition passed down by Severian of Gabala in Syria that Paul wrote Hebrews in Hebrew and that it was later translated by either Luke or Clement.[72] This tradition appears to date the late fourth century[73] and while it would explain some criticisms of the Pauline view, it also creates new problems for Pauline advocates. The first is why such a letter would need to be translated at all. It has been noted that Paul's command of the Greek language was such that "he would write a Greek letter without thought of employing a translator."[74] In fact, it is generally agreed that all of Paul's epistles were originally written by him in Greek. Why would Paul need a translator for Hebrews?

One might argue that the Greek translation was made after the fact for gentile converts but was never intended for its original recipients. This speculation appears logical on the surface, but is refuted by a number of Greek language experts who believe that the Greek of Hebrews utilizes "Greek Paranomosia (play on words)" and other phrases that prohibit the translation theory.[75] How? Let us examine one example. According to a number of these language experts, the opening words of Hebrews, "πολυμερως και πολυτροπως" [*polumeros kai polutropos*] allegedly have no equivalent in Hebrew or Aramaic.[76] They form an almost poetic introduction in Greek, but nothing in Hebrew can compare. Is this true? The English translation of those words is "in many times and in various ways." The Hebrew translation found in modern Hebrew New Testaments is, to be honest, somewhat rough. This does not rule out translation, but at best shows that the translator (if there was one) used a free handed translation which would be somewhat inconsistent with inerrancy.[77] We must, therefore, conclude that the translation theory is at best a possibility, but by no means a probability.

The most logical reason for the appearance of a Greek text written to Hebrews is that the author could not read and write Hebrew or Aramaic fluently. If this is the case, then Paul could not be the author.

Therefore, the "style" and vocabulary of Hebrews is insufficient to prove that Paul wrote the epistle. Nevertheless, we cannot invalidate Paul either. Such is usually the case in regard to "style" arguments.

Pauline Theology
Another argument is that the "theology" of Hebrews is strongly "Pauline." Now while this arguments has its merits, I have a number of problems with it. For one thing, there is only *one* Christian theology; that of Christ. It is true that theologians may emphasize different aspects of the gospel, or communicate the message of the gospel to different people in slightly different ways, but if the message is not the same, then it is not the gospel. The idea that "there was no single normative form of Christianity in the first century"[78] stems from the Tübingen school of thought (often called the "liberal" or "rationalist" scholars of German in the nineteenth century). According to them Peter taught a "Jewish Christianity" whereas Paul and Luke taught a "Hellenistic Christianity" which was in constant conflict with the teachings of Peter.[79] Of course, it is true that there was a debate, and some tension, over the question of circumcision (Acts 15; Galatians 2) but it is also true that Peter repented of his position (Acts 15:7-11) and after that time there is not the slightest hint of discord between Peter and Paul. In fact, Peter equates the epistles of

Paul with the Scriptures (2 Peter 3:15-16)! How is it then that David Wenham can argue in an evangelical text book that "Paul [was] the founder of Christianity as we know it and his religion being radically different from that of Jesus"![80] Despite this outrageous remark many evangelicals have come to use the same terminology as these heretics who claim that Christianity, as found in the epistles of Paul, is different from that of Christ upon which the religion of Christ is founded!

Let us consider, for example, the allegation that Paul's theology is a "Hellenistic Judaism." Because Paul opposed requiring circumcision for converts, he has been called a "Hellenistic" Jews. His ministry to gentiles is further used as evidence of this "Hellenism." However, any serious scholar knows that Paul minced no words when it came to condemning Greek Hellenism and philosophy (cf. 1 Corinthians 3:9). Indeed, many would say that Paul was far more "Jewish" than Peter (Galatians 2:14). He was a student of Gamaliel, the famed Pharisee teacher (Acts 22:3), and maintained many Jewish customs unto his dying day, even arguing that the gospel was to the Jews *first*, and only then to the gentiles (cf. Romans 1:16). Was Paul's "theology" really "Hellenistic"? For that matter, is Hebrews "Hellenistic"?

This hits at the crux of the problem. Hebrews is in many ways the most Jewish all the epistles. It has more quotations from the *Torah* than any other epistle and discusses in details the Jewish rituals and customs. The only thing "Hellenistic" about Hebrews is the fact that it quotes exclusively from the Greek

Septuagint (a translation of the Hebrew Bible). This, however, differs from Paul, for Paul's epistles often utilized his own translations from the Hebrew *Torah*, although occasionally using that of the Greek *Septuagint*. Notice how one scholar can call Hebrews "Hellenistic" while another calls it the most "Jewish" of the epistles. So also Paul is sometimes called "Hellenistic" even though he often mocks Hellenistic philosophy as "foolishness before God" (1 Corinthians 3:19).

Some have argued that the statement of Hebrews 10:38, "the just shall live by faith," is also found in Romans 1:17 and Galatians 3:11 but it is, in fact, a quotation from Habakkuk 2:4! This is not "Pauline theology" but *Biblical* theology.

Others have noted significant differences in "theology." For example some note that Hebrews entirely omits the debate over gentile circumcision which Paul had been so adamant about in some of his early epistles.[81] This, however, is topical, not theological. Moreover, the debate over circumcision had been long settled by the time Hebrews was written, so that the argument is neither evidence for or against Paul.

There are many other points of similarities and differences which I could cite, but this is pointless. First, there is *one* theology; that of Christ. Second, it is already well established that the author was a friend of Timothy (Hebrews 13:23) and therefore probably an acquaintance of Paul as well. Thus any similarities can be, and often are, used as evidence for any number of other candidates. The arguments from "theology" are a wash-out with the evidence neither proving nor disproving Paul's authorship.

Internal Biblical Evidence
The strongest evidence should be internal within the text of the epistle itself. Several passages have been used to either support or nullify Paul's authorship. The first is that of 2:3.

In Hebrews 2:3 the authors speaks of the gospel and says, "After it was at the first spoken through the Lord, it was confirmed to us by those who heard." He thus counts himself among those who had "heard" the gospel second hand, but a great many scholars have pointed out that Paul made emphasis of the fact that he was an apostle "not sent from men nor through the agency of man, but through Jesus Christ and God the Father, who raised Him from the dead" (Galatians 1:1). He further goes on to state that after God "revealed His Son in me so that I might preach Him among the Gentiles, I did not immediately consult with flesh and blood nor did I go up to Jerusalem to those who were apostles before me; but I went away to Arabia, and returned once more to Damascus. Then three years later I went up to Jerusalem" (1:15-18). This seems a far cry from one to whom "it was confirmed to us by those who heard" (2:3). Charles Erdman said that "the writer places himself among those to whom the gospel has been brought by men who heard the Lord ... (2:3) whereas Paul always maintains stoutly that he has received the gospel not 'from men, neither through men' but 'through revelation of Jesus Christ.'"[82] Despite this seeming conflict, John Ebrard declares that Hebrews

2:3 "nowise presents any hindrance to the supposition of the Pauline authorship."[83]

The second argument is from 10:32-34 wherein the author refers to the "former days" of conflict and suffering. Some have argued that this is a reference to Paul's persecution of Acts 8. Others have said "10:32-34 cannot refer to Saul's early oppression of the believers in Jerusalem and in Palestine because of the much later time at which the epistle was written."[84] Nevertheless, this is a subjective opinion either way. Whether it was specifically Paul's persecution or the persecution of other early oppressors is irrelevant for it would not prove who wrote Hebrews in either case. However, the translation of 10:34 could be of greater importance.

The King James Bible, and other translations based on the Majority text, read "ye had compassion of me in my bonds" (Hebrews 10:34). This would indicate that the author was in prison in Jerusalem, and thus make a strong argument for Paul (assuming the epistle was written to Jews in Israel).[85] The problem is that the most ancient texts read, with most modern translations, "you showed sympathy to the prisoners," indicating that the author was not one of the prisoners.

The possessive pronoun "my" is found in the famed Sinai Codex as well as the Majority text, and is quoted by Clement of Alexandria. However, there is no possessive pronoun found in Papyrus 46 ($\mathfrak{P}^{46}$ – arguably the oldest papyrus in existence) or the Codex Alexandria. It is also missing from the earliest Latin and Syrian translations. So while "my" is found in the Sinai Codex, the oldest manuscripts lack the possessive pronoun. Nonetheless, the deciding factor in the modern translations omitting "my" is its parallel in Hebrews 13:3 which may refer to the same individuals.[86] Consequently, 10:34 cannot be proof that the author was a prisoner in Jerusalem.

One final argument from within the text is the fact that the author appears to be a friend of Timothy (13:22-23). This certainly favors Paul, but is hardly conclusive since Timothy had many friends and acquaintances. At best it proves that the author was someone from within the "Pauline circle" of friends, but even that is suspect since most, if not all, of the surviving apostles doubtless knew Timothy as well. What is of more interest is the assertion of Zane Hodges that 13:23 suggest Paul had already died or else "Timothy might have been expected to join Paul."[87] This leads to the critical question. When did Paul meet his martyrdom?

Date of Paul's Death

In chapter one I already asserted that Timothy would never have been released by Nero. Paul's first imprisonment resulted in his release only because the great Stoic senator and advisor to Nero, Seneca, was ruling in Nero's name and most likely argued in Paul's favor. After 64 A.D., however, when Nero had forced Seneca to step down and after the fire in Rome, Nero did not even afford most Christians trials, regardless of their status. Some nobles may have received mock trials, but Nero's ferocity and barbarity left no Christian safe. Since we have already established that the Neronian persecution had begun, the only question is exactly when Paul had died.

Tradition and ancient historians differ on the exact year of Paul's death. Four dates have been variously given for Paul's execution. The first is that of Dionysius, a second century bishop of Corinth, who believed that Paul died with Peter in 65 A.D.,[88] the second is that of Aurelius Prudentius Clemens (a fourth century poet) who claimed that Paul died on the same date as Peter, but a year after,[89] the third view is that he died "two years later" in 67 A.D.,[90] and the last view is that he died in the "last year of Nero" which was 68 A.D.[91]

In *Apostles After Jesus* I gave a thorough critique of these views. I shall not repeat it here, but state my conclusion that Paul died on the same day as hundreds, perhaps thousands, of other Christians in 65 A.D.; a day Nero made a spectacle of the Christians. Nevertheless, even if we accept the latest possible date, that of 68 A.D., the fact that Timothy had already been released (13:23) indicates that Nero had already died, and therefore that Paul had already been martyred.

The Argument from Peter's Epistle
One additional argument has been put forth in favor of Paul which should be addressed before arriving at a conclusion. It has been argued by many that 2 Peter 3:15-16 confirms that Paul was the author of Hebrews. How? The argument is that Peter epistles were written to the Jews and that in 2 Peter 3:15-16 he states that "our beloved brother Paul ... wrote to you" as well. Since all of Paul's known epistles

"were addressed to churches of Gentiles"[92] it is argued that this *must* refer to the book of Hebrews.

The problems with this argument are many. First, while is assume that Peter was writing to Jews, it is undeniable that he was writing to the churches of "Pontus, Galatia, Cappadocia, Asia, and Bithynia" (1 Peter 1:1). Nowhere does it state that Peter was writing to the same recipients as Hebrews, and many argue to this very day about whom the recipients may have been. Some even dispute whether or not the "aliens" of 1 Peter 1:1 were Jews or not. That debate, however, is not necessary for the entire argument falls apart based solely on the fact that Peter was writing to, among others, "Galatia." One of Paul's epistles was "Galatians." In fact, almost all of Paul's epistles were written to the churches of Asia Minor, and it is *only* the churches of Asia Minor which are mentioned in 1 Peter 1:1. There is therefore no need to speculate upon whether Peter was referring to the epistle to the Hebrews. He was not.

Additional problems with this argument include the fact that Peter had almost certainly died before Hebrews was written. Others have pointed out that Paul called himself an apostle to the Gentiles, not Jews.[93] This last argument, however, is not particularly convincing since Paul continued to minister to "the Jew first" (Romans 1:16).

Conclusion
The evidence in favor of Paul is largely that of tradition and the connection to Timothy. Advocates, however, have a hard time explaining why Paul remained anonymous. The argument that Paul

withdrew his name because of hatred from Jews is not only weak, but as one pointed out, "Paul would not stoop to such a deception, and so crude a form of chicanery would never have been successful."[94] Although similarities in style and theology do exist, there are as many dissimilarities which nullify the evidence, making it neutral at best.

The evidence against Paul is more substantial. Western tradition, where one would expect the strongest support, was actually strongly against Pauline authorship for three hundred years. Hebrews 2:3 cast serious doubt upon Paul as well, since it is unthinkable that Paul would associate himself with being a second generation Christian (cf. Galatians 1:15-18). The failure to explain why Paul would deliberately withhold his name from the epistle is more than an argument from silence. Nevertheless, the strongest evidence is the weight of evidence dating Hebrews to the late sixties. If this is so, and even many Pauline advocates admit as much, then Paul would almost certainly have been dead. Even we accept the late date for Paul's martyrdom the release of Timothy from prison indicates that Nero had already died, and therefore so had Paul.

There is a reason that the epistle of Hebrews did not carry the name of Paul for centuries. Those translations which insert Paul's name are misleading. Even J. Vernon McGee, an advocate of Pauline authorship, states that "we deplore the fact that the King James Version carries the heading, The Epistle of Paul the Apostle to the Hebrews."[95] The facts indicate very strongly that Paul was almost certainly not the author of Hebrews, which is why no copy of Hebrews bore his name for centuries.

Chart on Theory of Pauline Authorship

Strengths	Neutral Arguments	Weaknesses
He was a Jew well versed in the Law.	Scholars are deeply divided over whether or not the style and vocabulary are Pauline.	Hebrews 2:3 seems to imply that the author never met Jesus, but Paul repeatedly and emphatically stated that he was personally called by Jesus.
There is a long tradition of Pauline authorship.	The argument from "Pauline theology" is inconclusive.	It is likely that Paul had already died under Neronian persecutions before Hebrews was written.
He spoke with authority for he was an apostle of Jesus Christ.		Assuming Hebrews is not a translation (as many believe), why would Paul have written in Greek at all?
He was well spoken and intellectual, more than capable of writing an masterful work like Hebrews.		Ancient western tradition rejected Pauline authorship for over 300 years, although this is where we would expect the strongest support, if he had written it from Rome.
He well educated in both Hebrew and Greek.		Why would Paul break from his tradition of signing all his epistles?
He was a close associate of Timothy.		

As the reader can see, while there are many positive arguments which can be made for Paul, the negative arguments against it are seemingly insurmountable, particularly if my dates for Paul's death and Hebrew's writing are correct. The arguments from style and "theology" are often touted as the strongest arguments in Paul's favor, but I consider them to be neutral arguments as the evidence is inconclusive.

Likelihood that Paul wrote Hebrews :
Doubtful but possible.

4

Suspect # 2 – Barnabas

After Paul there is no other candidate with as strong a tradition as that of Barnabas. "The name of Barnabas was apparently the first to be advanced"[96] and appears to have been considered by the western church to be a fact, rather than an opinion. Like Paul, there is ample support within the text for his authorship, but also like Paul there is good reason to reject it.

The Tradition of Barnabas
"Tertullian referred to [Barnabas' authorship] as a fact, not as an oral tradition."[97] The western church thus seemed to accept Barnabas as the author of Hebrews *at least* a few decades before the eastern church came to view Paul as the author. So sure were they that the famous Bible Codex Claremontanus gives Hebrews the title "the epistle of Barnabas."[98] This epistle should not be confused with the so-called "epistle of Barnabas" found among the pseudepigrapha. On the contrary, the Codex contains an ancient catalogue of canonical books. Missing is the "book of Hebrews" but in its place stands "the epistle of Barnabas." As with Tertullian, the quotations from this "epistle of Barnabas" are not from the spurious pseudepigrapha of Barnabas (see below) but the book of Hebrews mislabeled as the "epistle of Barnabas."[99] Hence it is clear that the western church believed Barnabas wrote the epistle.

"The Epistle of Barnabas"
The aforementioned pseudepigraphal "epistle of Barnabas" (not Hebrews) is dated sometime between the destruction of the Temple in 70 A.D. (to which it refers) and before the Bar Kochba revolt of 132 A.D. Most date it to approximately 100 A.D.[100] Some believe that it was authored by Barnabas of Alexandria, a now forgotten Apostolic Father who has been confused with the Biblical Barnabas.[101] This is not surprising for it is said that after the martyrdom of the Biblical Barnabas in Cyprus, his cousin Mark fled to the safety of Alexandria.[102] Hence, those who mistakenly believed Barnabas was still alive in the later half of the first century would naturally assume that Barnabas traveled with Mark to Alexandria. In fact, Barnabas had died sometime in the 50s.[103]

Nevertheless, this epistle bears some similarities to the book of Hebrews, which has heightened speculation that they may have been written by the same person. However, the similarities are not substantial but rather superficial. For example, Barnabas 4:3 mentions Enoch, Barnabas 8 calls the red heifer as a type of Christ, and Barnabas 16 discusses the temple (and its destruction). It is the latter which is of most interest to scholars. One author notes that "the Maccabaean spirit of the Jews never burned more furiously than after the destruction of Jerusalem."[104] He believes that the epistle of Barnabas was written to Christian Jews in whom this same spirit was kindled, and urges them to reject the old temple for a "spiritual" temple in our hearts (Barnabas 6:15; 16:10).

Despite the clear similarities, there are marked differences in the epistles, particularly in regard to their theology. While Hebrews emphasizes Jesus as the typological fulfillment of the Tabernacle, the epistle of Barnabas emphasized the "spiritual" temple (Barnabas 6:15; 16:10). Jesus as High Priest is the focus of Hebrews, but the epistle of Barnabas focuses upon the New Covenant, which he believes signals the abolishment of the old. Indeed, there is a strong attack against Judaizers in this Barnabas. In one passage he even suggest that the New Covenant has no application to the Jews (cf. Barnabas 13:1), whereas Hebrews 8:10 makes clear that the New Covenant, although not restricted to Jews, was "made with the house of Israel."

In short, the epistle of Barnabas was written after the Biblical Barnabas had already died. It shows that the book of Hebrews was already well known and accepted at the end of the first century, but proves nothing else. The similarities are due to the influence of Hebrews and nothing more.

"Style" and Vocabulary

As with all candidates the "style" of the epistle is variously argued to be consistent with, or opposed to, a certain author. Barnabas is no exception. The irony here, however, is that there is no extant writing of Barnabas with which to compare! Those who argue that the "style" of Hebrews is incompatible with that of the pseudepigraphal "epistle of Barnabas" nullify their own argument. H.A. Ironside, for example, states that "if it should be proved that Barnabas were the author of the properly spurious epistle ascribed to him, the difference in style ... is too marked."[105] So in one breath he admits that the "epistle of Barnabas" a "spurious epistle," thereby admitting it was not written by the Biblical Barnabas, but then turns around and argues that the differences in style are "too marked" to have been written by the same person! So critics destroy their own argument.

The so-called "epistle of Barnabas" to which Hebrews is compared was written after the destruction of the Temple[106] and long after the Biblical Barnabas was dead. Comparisons are therefore irrelevant and useless. We can say nothing of Barnabas' style other than that Barnabas was an eloquent man as suggested in Acts 4:36 and that such eloquence is consistent with the style of Hebrews.

Biblical Evidence

A variety of arguments for and against Barnabas have been proposed from Biblical evidence. The fact that Barnabas was Levite (Acts 4:36) is said to fit very well with the emphasis upon Levitical priesthood. Indeed, the Levites were the priestly caste in Israel, so it is natural that they would share an interest in the priesthood.

Other have tried to make a connection between Hebrew 13:22, the "word of exhortation," and the fact that Barnabas was a nickname meaning "son of exhortation" (Acts 4:36).[107] Certainly Barnabas was known for his eloquence, but the connection is tenuous.

Another piece of evidence is the close relationship which Barnabas shared with Paul. He would probably have known Timothy and would have shared much in common with the "Pauline theology" of Hebrews.

On the negative side Lenski argues that the leaders of the church to whom Hebrews was written had presumably died (13:7) and therefore the writer could not have been the founder of the church in question.[108] Of course, this begs the question of whether or not Barnabas could be considered the founder of the church in question. Since we cannot even say definitively where the church was located, it seems forced to argue that Barnabas was its founder. So Lenski's argument is invalid.

Finally, some critics note that if the epistle was written from Italy (13:24) then it most likely could not have been Barnabas for it was written "where it doth not appear that Barnabas ever was."[109] Now there is an ancient tradition which claims that Barnabas did indeed preach in Rome, but that tradition is suspect as it places Barnabas in Rome during the reign of Tiberius,[110] a time when he was most certainly with Paul in Asia.[111] Consequently, there is no evidence that Barnabas ever went to Rome.

The Date of Barnabas' Death

Like many of our candidates Barnabas died a martyr. Exactly when he died is critical in determining whether or not he could be the author of Hebrews.

Scholars are deeply divided upon when Barnabas's death occurred. It is generally agreed that he was dragged to his place of execution and then burned alive,[112] but some place this event in 64 A.D. shortly before the death of Paul,[113] while others, like John Foxe, place it as late as 73 A.D.[114] In the *Apostles After Jesus* I came to the conclusion that neither are acceptable. According to the traditions Mark fled from Cyprus escaping the same fate as Barnabas and went to Alexandria where he is credited with founding the church of Alexandria. This, however, could not have taken place later than the 50s, for Mark is found with Peter and Paul in the 60s and the church of Alexandria was already flourishing in the 70s. Additionally, the lack of any evidence of Barnabas's activities after his return to Cyprus (Acts 15:39) either in the Bible or in tradition, suggest that Barnabas met his death much earlier. Finally, Paul mentions Barnabas in 1 Corinthians 9:6 but fails to mention him in any epistle written thereafter, despite greeting his cousin Mark and other common companions. These facts lead me to believe that Barnabas died around 55 A.D.[115]

Conclusion
There was a time when Barnabas was my favorite candidate. Certainly the early western church appears to have favored Barnabas as the author and a few modern scholars, such as Zane Hodges still favor him,[116] but my opinions changed when I researched my history of the apostles. I can find no evidence that Barnabas survived beyond the mid-fifties. He was one of the earliest leaders to have been martyred and he almost certainly never made it to Rome, from which the epistle appears to have been written. It is

therefore unlikely that Barnabas wrote Hebrews, unless I err in both the date of this death and my search for evidence that he ever left Cyprus.

Chart on Theory of Barnabas' Authorship

Strengths	Neutral Arguments	Weaknesses
Western tradition strongly supports Barnabas.	It is not known whether or not Barnabas was a second generation Christian, but he likely was not (cf. Acts 4:36, 9:27).	He was almost certainly dead long before Hebrews was written.
Barnabas was a Levite who would be well versed in Tabernacle rituals and Levitical laws.		There is no evidence that Barnabas ever went to Italy.
Barnabas was known as a man of exhortation (Acts 4:36) and capable of writings Hebrews.		
Barnabas would have known Greek.		
He was a part of the Pauline circle and would have been familiar with Pauline theology.		
He would most likely have known Timothy.		
He was well respected and would have had authority to speak to the Jews if Israel.		

Although the evidence in favor of Barnabas far outnumbers the weaknesses, the weight of evidence against it far outweighs the evidence in favor. Strongest is the mass of evidence that Barnabas died in Cyprus sometime in the 50s, more than fifteen years before Hebrews was written.

Likelihood that Barnabas wrote Hebrews :
Highly doubtful.

5

Suspect # 3 – Luke

Luke is not one of whom most people think when they are thinking of the author of Hebrews, but he is actually one of the more formidable candidates, or is he? Traditionally Luke has been viewed as a translator of Hebrews, with the original author being Paul.[117] Some have favored Luke as the actual author himself. Most recently my former professor wrote a very large book proclaiming Luke the sole author of Hebrews. Is this so? Let us examine the facts.

Was It a Translation?
No tradition attributes Luke as the original author of Hebrews, but a great many ancients in the eastern church coupled the Pauline view with a translation by Luke. This was the view of Clement of Alexandria, Eusebius, Jerome, Theodoret, and many others.[118] So also Aquinas, in the middle ages, gave voice to the view,[119] and Reformer John Calvin believed it was possible, if not probable.[120] Given the closeness of Paul and Luke, it perhaps is natural to assume that Luke would translate Paul, but there are good reasons to reject it.

The first reason is simply the fact that "Paul is as versatile in Greek as he is in Aramaic, and he would write a Greek letter without thought of employing a translator."[121] If Hebrews was translated at all, we expect that it would be translated long after Paul's death. Since Luke survived Paul by several decades, we shall at least leave the door open for this possibility.

A second argument is that the Greek of Hebrews could not be a translation from Aramaic or Hebrew. The argument is that the "subtle play on words and the striking expressions found throughout the epistle all point toward the definite fact that the Greek text is the original one."[122] For example, the opening words are "πολυμερως και πολυτροπως" [*polumeros kai polutropos*] which allegedly has no equivalent in Hebrew or Aramaic.[123] This is, of course, an overstatement. The Hebrew translations found in Hebrew New Testaments today certain are not as "poetic" as the Greek and the "Greek Paranomosia (play on words)"[124] are not evident in Hebrew, but does this prove that no Hebrew ever existed? Could not a skilled translator have translated Hebrews more freely? Two things speak against this proposition. First, the inerrancy of the Bible tends to frown upon free translations which may tamper with the original meaning, and second, no Hebrew text has ever been found, nor are there any ancient traditions before Clement of Alexandria's time. Although by no means a settled issue, one is prone to reject the translation theory.

Still one other angle may be pursued. Some argued that if Luke did not translate Paul, then perhaps Paul supervised its writing under Luke. This is yet another attempt to wed the Pauline and Lukan traditions. Since Paul wrote many letters on his own to many churches, it remains a mystery why he would supervise a letter by Luke. Consequently, such speculation must be rejected without evidence.

"Style" and Vocabulary

If Luke did not translate Hebrews, might he have written it? This is the belief of David Allen. He devotes nearly 100 pages to outlining similarities between Luke-Acts and Hebrews, but others have just as weighty arguments against it. I have already expressed my discontent with too heavy an emphasis upon "style" and vocabulary arguments. Nevertheless, they are not without their uses. To that end Dr. Allen notes that there are 34% similarities between the nouns used in Luke and Hebrews[125] and 35% of the verbs are used in both Luke and Hebrews.[126] Combining both Luke and Acts, he then suggest that there is as much as 67% of the vocabulary in Luke and Acts common to that found in Hebrews.[127] My response is that 99% of my vocabulary is found in Websters' Dictionary.

Despite the seeming strength of Allen's analysis, I am inclined to agree with Warwick Allen of Dallas Theological Seminary who said that "such arguments are to be regarded warily, however, for the same process of reasoning could also be used to show that Luke was the author of the Epistle to the Colossians."[128] To the casual reader, even in Greek, it does not seem that Luke and Acts were written by the same man as Hebrews. When I examine style I do not do a careful analysis of verbs and nouns, but a casual reading. To me *that* is the basis of style far more so than nouns and verbs which may be common to people of a similar background and/or education. I will therefore allow the reader to read Luke, Acts, and Hebrews and reach his own judgment on this matter.

The "Theology" of Hebrews

Another argument is that the theology of Luke and Acts is similar to that of Hebrews.[129] Furthermore, as a companion of Paul he too would have shared common views with Paul in regard to theology. As before, I am suspect of distinguishing too greatly between Pauline theology, Petrine theology, and/or Lukan theology, for there is really only the theology of Christ. Common threads and points of emphasis are to be expected.

Now the critic will claim that I am being superficial and that any trained "scholar" will see the differences in theology, but I too am a "scholar" with a Ph.D. and there are as many who argue against Lukan theology as for Lukan theology. This alone demonstrates that the "theological" angle is by no means conclusive. We can say that Luke was consistent with the theology of Hebrews, but we cannot say more.

Finally, before we can say that Luke's "theology" is the same as that of Hebrews we must resolve the question of whether or not Luke was a Jew, for there is no book more thoroughly Jewish than Hebrews, and it has been the commonly held belief that Luke was a gentile. If so then we would have a hard time believing that Hebrews was Lukan in nature, and more importantly that a gentile could lecture Jews, and probably priests among them, upon Levitical law.

Jew or Gentile?

The dominant view in modern scholarship, whether evangelical, liberal, or moderate, is that Luke was a gentile convert to Judaism. However, no extant church father called Luke a gentile until Jerome. While this may be an argument from silence, for they also did not call Luke a Jew, it does open the door for the obvious question. Was Luke a Jew or gentile?

First, I will address the arguments that support Luke being a gentile. Aside from the long, if late, tradition passed on through the ages, it has been noted that in Colossians Paul states that Aristarchus, Mark, and Jesus called Justus "are the only fellow workers for the kingdom of God who are from the circumcision," or Jews (4:10-11). Paul then mentions Epaphras, Luke, and Demas who must have been gentiles (4:12-14) since Aristarchus, Mark, and Jesus called Justus were the "only" Jews among his "fellow workers."[130] Because Luke was obviously a "fellow worker" (v. 11) but not listed among the Jews, it is natural to assume he was a gentile. The only answer given to this is the statement that Luke was not a "fellow worker" but "was rather Paul's personal physician and historian."[131] This seems grasping at straws. As a matter of fact one author admits that the Luke of Colossians is a gentile, but then argues that this is a "different" Luke from the author of Luke and Acts.[132] He presents no evidence, but assumes it cannot be the same Luke, since he believes Luke to be a Jew.

Another argument is that Luke itself is a gentile name. However, I must agree with those who say that this is not a good argument for the Jews often went by different names, and even Paul is not a Hebrew name. In fact, when I worked with a Messianic Synagogue a few years back I was somewhat surprised to see that they refused to call Paul by his Christian name, instead referring to him as Saul. Nevertheless, Paul considered himself a new man after Christ and chose the new name just as Abram became Abraham and Sarai became Sarah. Consequently, it is not valid to argue someone's ethnicity based on names alone. My own name, David, actually Jewish although I am a gentile.

The arguments in favor of Luke being a Jew are as follows. First, Thomas McCall argues that Paul would never have used a gentile to preach the gospel because the Jews were the ones entrusted with the Word of God.[133] Indeed they were, but if we conclude from this that gentiles could not preach or that Paul would not allow them to preach, even though he refer to several gentile workers (such as in Colossians 4) then we would have to reject Paul's entire epistles, especially where he speaks out against the Judaizers who required gentiles to convert to Judaism before converting to Christ!

A second argument is that in Acts 21:29 Paul was falsely accused of bringing a gentile into the Temple because "they had previously seen Trophimus the Ephesian in the city with him" (21:29). It is thus argued that Luke, who is *assumed* to have been with him at the time (based on Acts 21:17), must have been a Jew since he was not mentioned.[134] Note the word *assumed*. This is an argument from silence. This is especially true since Luke never once mentions himself by name in the book of Acts! Was

Luke there? If he was there would he have inserted himself into the story, when he never does anywhere else? Let the reader judge for himself.

Next it is argued that Luke had "intimate knowledge of the Temple" based on Luke 1:8-20.[135] This statement is forced, however, for Luke was a historian. It is not surprising that he would get some basic knowledge about the Temple and there is nothing in Luke 1:8-20 which any gentile would be unaware of if he had done even minimal research.

Additionally McCall argues that Luke's personal relationship with Mary, of whom he wrote many anecdotes (cf. Luke 2:42-51), proves he was a Jew for it must have been "difficult ... for Gentiles to have gotten to the 'inner circle.'"[136] Again he is grasping at straws. Would Mary really have refused to discuss Jesus with "Paul's historian" because he was a gentile?

David Allen presents a far better argument, if not thoroughly convincing. He argues that Luke and Lucius are the same name and person. Thus he assumes that the Lucius of Acts 13:1 is Luke and since Romans 16:21 identifies Lucius as a "kinsman," then Luke must have been a Jew.[137] Unfortunately, this has several problems. To start with Lucius is described as a Cyrene (Acts 13:1) whereas Luke is believed to have come from Antioch.[138] Although there is no Bible passage to prove which is correct, there is not a single tradition of which I am aware that Luke was a Cyrene, but rather a native of Antioch. Additionally, Paul clearly calls him Luke in Colossians (4:14), 2 Timothy (4:11), and Philemon

(1:24), so we might wonder which he would call him Lucius in Romans. This is intriguing but speculative.

In short, Colossians 4:10-11 seems to support that Luke was a gentile, but this is somewhat balanced out by Acts 21:17-29. Neither is conclusive, but I believe that Colossians 4:10-11 is the stronger verse (despite the plethora of sarcasm from those who disagree). Thus it is probable that Luke was the only gentile to write a book of the Bible, showing God's grace and perhaps prophetically demonstrating the beginning of the Church age during the time of Israel's chastisement. I have no doubt that God will restore Israel (he has already restored part of the land), but the fact is that in this current dispensation the church is predominantly gentile with only a small remnant of God's chosen people.

The real irony of this debate is that it creates a paradox for those who believe Luke wrote Hebrews. If Luke was a gentile then it would explain why he would write a *Greek* letter to *Jewish* recipients. If, however, he was Jewish, then we cannot comprehend why he would have written in Greek. Moreover the paradox does not end there, for if Luke was not Jewish then he almost certainly did not write Hebrews, the most Jewish book of the New Testament, but in trying to make Luke a Jew (which is possible) they create the virtually insurmountable problem of explaining why he wrote in Greek.

Biblical Evidences
Biblical evidences should be the most important, but like the other candidates, we have only a few hints. Franz Delitzsch list four evidences. First, he draws a

parallel between 2 Timothy 4:11 and Hebrews 13:23. I will let the reader judge if such evidence is worthy or not. Second, He notes that Luke had been to Jerusalem (Acts 21:17). Third, he believes that Luke may have been a Jew. Fourth, he notes that the author of Hebrews may have a medical background based on Hebrews 4:12; 5:12-14 and 12:12.[139]

The first point is highly suspect. The second point is valid. The third point has been debated already, but I will acquiesce to the belief that he was a Jew for the sake of argument. The fourth point is most worthy of discussion.

Hebrews 4:12 reads, "For the word of God is living and active and sharper than any two-edged sword, and piercing as far as the division of soul and spirit, of both joints and marrow, and able to judge the thoughts and intentions of the heart." This is a beautiful passage, but does it really prove "anatomical" knowledge?[140] Likewise, Hebrews 5:12-14 describes the recipients as "need[ing] milk and not solid food." This, it is said, shows "dietetical" concern.[141] Really? Lastly, it is said that Hebrews 12:12 shows a therapeutical concern as it reads, "strengthen the hands that are weak and the knees that are feeble."[142] Again, I will let the reader decide if these passages demonstrate a medical background or not.

Conclusion
In many ways Luke is a promising candidate. He was certainly more the fluent in Greek and his meticulous research makes him a valid candidate for the author of Hebrews. Unlike the previous candidates Luke

was definitely still alive when Hebrews was written, and he was probably a friend of Timothy through their mutual friend Paul. Unfortunately, the strengths end here.

Luke may or may not have been a Jew, but probably was not, as tradition holds and as Colossians 4:10-11 strongly implies. Moreover, if he was a Jew then he would certainly have known Hebrew so it makes no sense for him to have written Hebrews in Greek. This is the great irony of Lukan theorists. A gentile would probably not be able to read Hebrew and thus rely on the *Septuagint* while writing in Greek, but a Jew would certainly know Hebrew or Aramaic (they were taught the language[s] from childhood). In addition, I urge the reader to read through Luke-Acts and through Hebrews. You do not need to be a Greek scholar to see that the style cannot definitively be said to be the same.

In short, the evidence for Luke is relatively meager. He *could* have been the author, but there is little evidence that he did, and some good evidence he did not. If we balance the scales, then we would have to decide against Luke.

Chart on Theory of Lukan Authorship

Strengths	Neutral Arguments	Weaknesses
Luke was a member of Paul's inner circle.	Arguments from style and vocabulary are inconclusive.	Luke was probably a gentile proselyte (cf. Colossians 4:10-14).
Luke was fluent in Greek and could easily have written the Greek of Hebrews.	Arguments from "theology" are inconclusive.	
Luke almost certainly knew Timothy.	The tradition that Luke translated Hebrews has only limited appeal to the alleged authorship.	
Luke was alive when Hebrews was written.	It is unknown how much authority Luke would have had in Israel.	
Luke was probably a second generation Christian.		

Luke has few weaknesses *per se*, but many questionable evidences. Those arguments in his favor may also be found among any number of other candidates, so while Luke may not be ruled out, there is nothing about Luke which truly makes him stand out as the likely author of Hebrews.

Likelihood that Luke wrote Hebrews :
Possible, but not likely.

6

Suspect # 4 – Apollos

Apollos is mentioned twice in Acts, several times in 1 Corinthians, and once in Titus. His name is never mentioned in any known tradition concerning Hebrews until Martin Luther's famous aside "this Apollos was a man of high understanding, the Epistle of the Hebrews is indeed his."[143] Luther then says nothing more about him, but many have. In fact, Apollos has risen to become one of the most popular candidates despite relatively little evidence for or against him. Perhaps it is because there is as little against him that his appeal has increased for we have seen that the favorite candidates, while having ample supporting evidence, all have fatal flaws (such as being dead).

Acts 18:24 states "now a Jew named Apollos, an Alexandrian by birth, an eloquent man, came to Ephesus; and he was mighty in the Scriptures." This is the verse used as the primary support for "an eloquent man" who was "mighty in the Scriptures" would certainly be capable of writing Hebrews. Moreover, as an associate of Paul (1 Corinthians 3:6) he would certainly be familiar with "Pauline theology" and probably be an acquaintance of Timothy.

Another argument in Apollos's favor is that he heard the gospel second hand from Paul (Acts 19:1-6) which fits perfectly with Hebrews 2:3. Yet another piece of evidence is the fact that Apollos was an

Alexandrian (Acts 18:24) which could explain the exclusive quotations from the Greek *Septuagint*, which was written in Alexandria, Egypt.

One author suggests that Apollos did not sign the epistle because his name would have been offensive to Jews, for he was named after the pagan god Apollo![144] While this is feasible, it is not necessary for John did not sign any of his three epistles. The failure to sign the epistle is only relevant if the author is known to have customarily signed his epistles. Some authors merely sign their name to the seal (think of an ancient envelope) so the recipients of the epistle certainly knew who wrote them even if we do not.

It is also said that Apollos must have been a man of prominence and importance since his name is mentioned alongside Paul, Peter, and Jesus in 1 Corinthians 1:12.[145] Obviously the author of Hebrews was someone of prominence recognized by the community there. This too fits Apollos (albeit many others as well).

Against Apollos is the universal silence of tradition. H.A. Ironside noted that "it is strange, if Apollos were the author, that the Alexandrian church never seems to have heard of it, and yet Apollos was of Alexandria."[146] Indeed, the Alexandrian church was the church which supported Pauline authorship, but if one of their own had written Hebrews it would indeed seem odd that not a single extant voice was ever raised in support of Apollos. Moreover, Aiken believes that Clement of Rome knew Apollos personally, but did not identify Apollos as the author of Hebrews.[147]

On the surface Apollos seems to have strong support and only one major problem, being a lack of tradition. For this reason Apollos has become a popular candidate.[148] One advocate declares that he is "the least unlikely of the conjectures."[149] This, of course, is not exactly a glowing endorsement. The problem is that while there is only one major drawback, there is no solid evidence for it which could not be equally said of a number of other candidates. Apollos is thus a possibility, but we cannot say more.

Chart on Theory of Apollos' Authorship

Strengths	Neutral Arguments	Weaknesses
He was an Alexandrian who would have been versed in the *Septuagint* and fluent in Greek.	We have no information on Apollos' ministry or death after the book of Acts.	There is not a single tradition of Apollos's authorship for 1500 years.
He was "mighty in the Scriptures" and a solid speaker (cf. Acts 18:24).	He may have been a second generation Christian since he need instruction, but we cannot know for sure.	
He was an associate of Paul.	It is unknown if he had ever been to Rome.	
He probably knew Timothy.		
He was a Jew.		

While Apollos has become a favorite because of the few negatives against him, the reader can plainly see how many question marks remain. We know less about Apollos than most of the other serious candidates, which makes it hard to either eliminate him ... or to say that he was the author.

Likelihood that Apollos wrote Hebrews :
Possible, but unknown.

7

Suspect # 5 – Priscilla and Aquila

Priscilla (or Prisca) and Aquila were friends of Paul whom he met in Corinth after Claudius expelled Jew from Rome (18:2-26). They became traveling companions and associates of Paul. In his epistles Paul showed an affection for Priscilla whom he referred to by her nickname Prisca. By all accounts Priscilla and Aquila were a godly couple who ministered together as husband and wife.

Like Apollos there is not a single tradition of either one in regard to the book of Hebrews. However, in the early twentieth century the Tübingen scholar (the original liberal theologians – and such they called themselves) Adolph von Harnack suggested that Priscilla might be the author.[150] He says nary a word about Aquila, but emphasized Priscilla. This view was rejected by most until it was picked up by some modern "evangelical feminists."

The view does have some merit, but many problems; some insurmountable problems. Its popularity in recent years seems more motivated by modern day politics than Biblical exegesis as will become evident, but is deserving a full discussion and debate before rendering a verdict.

A Feminine Book?
First, it is impossible to debate this issue without discussing the politics (yes, politics) of modern feminism. Let me begin by saying that a female

author does not bother me in the least bit. However, some appear deeply disturbed if there was *not* a female author in the Bible. This is nowhere more obvious that Ruth Hoppin's assertion that "Hebrews appears to be the product of a feminine mind."[151] She then sets out, like Harnack, to create a "psychological construct"[152] to prove this.

She argues that the champions of faith cited in the famous eleventh chapter of Hebrews includes several women, including the prostitute Rahab (11:31). She then argues that a man would not have listed such people.[153] Of course, one author responded that the same reasoning must prove that James was a woman since he too praises Rahab (James 2:25). Or even that Luke must have been a woman for the sympathetic portrayals of women found in Luke and Acts![154] It seems more than a little sexist to claim that men do not respect and honor women like Rahab.

Additionally, Hoppin goes on to argue that the author shows "compassion," "purity," "empathy," and "sympathy" which, according her, indicate a female author.[155] Once again, we would have to conclude then that Jesus was a woman and that all men are unsympathetic impure cold hearted Cretans? Such a "psychological construct" only shows the politics of modern feminism. Christianity produces "compassion," "purity," "empathy," and "sympathy." To suggests that these are feminine characteristics is more than sexism, but borderline blasphemy. These are not masculine or feminine virtues. They are godly virtues.

Harold Copping – The Tent Makers – 1907

In another place Hoppin argues that the phrase "I have written you briefly" should be properly translated "written a little" as a way of apologizing. Her argument is that a woman would be more apologetic for her letter given the law against women preaching or teaching men.[156] Firstly, the most literal translation would be "through brief words." It is true that the letter does not seem to be short, but context is the key. The author is dealing with a subject that requires a long discourse, so in that context it is short.

To imply that this is evidence of gender is a stretch to say the least.

The greatest, and insurmountable, problem with the "feminine construct" is the fact that Hebrews 11:32 uses a masculine participle. What does this mean? In many languages, such as Greek, verbs carry gender. In English we simply say "he tells," "she tells," or "I tell," but when using the first person, "I tell" we cannot know if the author is male or female. In Greek, however, you can. The word in question is διηγουμενον (*di'egoumenon*) which is translated "I will be telling," or more simply "I tell." In Greek it is *masculine*, identifying the speaker as a man.

The only answer Hoppin can give is to suggest either that "she wanted to conceal who she was"[157] and therefore lied, deliberately using the wrong verb, or that it may have originally been feminine and was changed by some man later.[158] The first answer would nullify Hebrews from the sacred Scriptures since deceit and lies are contrary to the teaching of Jesus and the Mosaic Law. To argue that the Bible was written in a deceptive or dishonest way, with no evidence to support it, is to show contempt for the Scriptures. The second answer is no better since every manuscript ever found dating back to papyrus 46 ($\mathfrak{P}^{46}$), a copy most likely dating to a time when John and Mark were still living (see *Controversies in the Gospels* for my defense of this), are the same. Not a single manuscript shows any hint of alteration. Hoppin must, like her mentor of the Tübingen school, *assume* the Bible to be error without evidence to support it.

The Anonymity

The Priscilla view does offer a feasible argument for the alleged anonymity of the letter, if a suspect one. Harnack argued that the identity of author was suppressed "intentionally" to avoid knowledge that it was written by a woman,[159] while Hoppin takes the slightly less moderated view that Priscilla herself withheld her name fearing that "disclosure of the author's identity was bound to result in rejection of the letter."[160] The former suggest a male conspiracy after the fact while the later suggest that Priscilla attempted to deceive her audience in order to hide her identity.

Although these arguments may sound like a plausible explanation they are very weak. Aside from the unethical angle of deception, there are several logical problems. Harnack argued that the Codex Bezae betrays an anti-woman bias, thus supporting his thesis but his actual evidence consist of nothing more than the fact that Aquila's name appears before Priscilla's name in Acts 18:26. He ignores the fact that many other manuscripts, including the Majority text, also contain Aquila's name first. Even if it is proven true that the names were deliberate invades, which he has not done, this is a far cry from proving gender bias. The inversion of names is a very common mistake found in textual criticism and rarely if ever relevant.

Another problem with the view is simple logic. If Priscilla wrote the letter with her husband, to whom they appeal in problem passages, then why wouldn't he have simply signed *his* name? Was he not co-author of the letter? Why withhold your name instead of allowing your husband and co-author to sign it? The arguments, therefore, fall apart upon closer examination and prove nothing about the author of Hebrews. The reasoning is forced.

Multiple Authors?
One popular argument used in support of Priscilla is the fact that the letter sometimes uses the pronoun "I" (11:32; 13:19, 22) while at other times referring to "us" and "we" (13:18)[161] This, it is argued, proves two authors, rather than just one. Now while it may seem a promising argument on the surface, it has several problems.

The first problem is that fact that Paul also uses "we" and "us" countless times throughout his epistles, as well as the singular "I" and "me." The use of "we" and/or "us" may refer to other members of the church, or it may be generic for Christians as a whole, depending on the context. In the case of Hebrews the appearance of the plural "we" most likely refers to the church members of whom he mentions in 13:24. Since this is the postscript of the letter it is by no means unusual or uncommon and proves nothing whatsoever in regard to the author.

The second problem is that the argument is self defeating, for even if the epistle was written by a husband and wife team, then why should Priscilla get the credit? Might not Aquila have been the primary author, since the masculine verb is used for the writer? To answer this argument Harnack and Hoppin argue that because Paul lists Priscilla's name first, she must have been the leader,[162] but this response is inherently weak.

Of the six times Priscilla and Aquila are mentioned in the Bible Priscilla's name appear first in four of those. Paul, however, refers to her as Prisca which infers an intimacy of friendship. Consequently, it is likely that Paul and Luke were close friends with Priscilla and her name appears first out of respect to their friendship. Alternately it has been suggested that this is a chivalrous custom, like saying "ladies and gentleman." In no way can it be argued that this depicts supremacy.

Despite this fact, Harnack and Hoppin argue that Acts 18:26 proves that "Priscilla was the primary teacher"[163] of Apollos based solely on the fact that her name appears before Aquila's! Thus they argue that Priscilla violated her friend, and apostle, Paul's command which forbids a woman to teach a man on spiritual matters (1 Timothy 2:12).[164] Once again, it is idle speculation at best. Nothing in the Bible proves that Aquila was Priscilla's subordinate, and to make this claim would actually violate numerous commands by both Peter and Paul concerning husband and wife relationships (cf. 1 Peter 3:1; Ephesians 5:22; Colossians 3:18; 1 Timothy 2:12). They were a couple. They were husband and wife. They were a team. Nothing in the Scriptures proves Priscilla to be Aquila's superior, and nothing proves that more than one person wrote Hebrews, let alone that it must have been Priscilla *if* a husband and wife team did write it.

Additional Arguments
Now although I have been highly critical of the evidences so far this view is not without some good arguments. For example, it is apparent that Priscilla and Aquila were very well versed and learned. They understood the word of God and even instructed Apollos (Acts 18:24-26). In this respect *they* fit the criteria.

Moreover, it is clear that Priscilla and Aquila were a part of the Pauline inner circle and almost certainly acquaintances of Timothy. This also supports the alleged "Pauline theology" found in Hebrews, while also accounting for the differences.

Furthermore, if Hebrews was written from Italy as Hebrews 13:24 suggest, then Priscilla and Aquila would again fit very well, for they were originally from Rome, having been evicted under the Edict of Claudius in 49 A.D. (Acts 18:2).

While all these evidences favor Priscilla *and* Aquila, Hoppin and Harnack once again overplay their hand. Not content to accept the evidence at face value, Hoppin goes to great length to argue Priscilla was a convert of Peter who she says came to Rome in 42-43 A.D.[165] She produces several chapters proving that Peter had been in Rome, and probably knew Priscilla, but does not present one iota of evidence for her 42 A.D. date which even many Catholics reject. For example, Catholic historian Bernard Ruffin appears to place the arrival of Peter in Rome sometime between 50 and 57 A.D.[166] Indeed, with the exception of Paul, the book of Acts does not depict any of the apostles leaving Israel before the Council of Jerusalem, which may be dated to around

49 A.D.[167] In my own research, I concluded that Peter probably did not reach Rome until 63 or 64 A.D.[168]

Still this is not enough for Hoppin. She attempts to build a case for the idea that Hebrews was written to Ephesus, which she believes supports Priscilla since they had journeyed there with Paul at one time.[169] The reason she devotes so much space to this argument is because if Hebrews was written to an Israeli congregation, then it is not as likely that Priscilla and Aquila would have been well known there, and as a result would not have had the authority which the epistle's author clearly carries. The case for Ephesus, however, is not a strong one (see Chapter 2).

So it can be said in favor of Priscilla and Aquila that they were educated, intelligent, known in Rome, and acquaintances of Timothy and Paul. It is not likely, however, they were known in Israel and the conjecture of Ephesus is probably not the letter's destination as it had a majority gentile population and offers no solid credible evidence on its behalf.

The Death of Priscilla and Aquila
One final examination needs to be that of the death of Priscilla and Aquila. I have already shown that several of the candidates were probably dead by the time Hebrews was written. Indeed, the epistle's reference to "former days" (10:32) and the passing of its leaders (13:7) indicates that many of the early church leaders (and even a number of the apostles) had already passed on to heaven. Were Priscilla and Aquila among those already dead?

This is not an easy question because the traditions of Priscilla and Aquila are divided. Most traditions say that they died under Nero's persecutions, but one claims that they traveled with Luke after Nero's death.[170] In *The Apostles After Christ* I reached the conclusion that the majority of traditions were stronger than the one that places him with Luke. This is not only because of the weight of traditions (which can be wrong) but because of their prominence in Rome. As leaders of the Roman church it is highly unlikely that they would have escaped the eye of Nero.[171] In fact, of all the Biblical leaders who were in Rome during the persecutions only Clement, Timothy, Luke, and Mark appear to have escaped death (although the famed *Babylon Namebook* does claim Mark died under Nero[172]). All the others appear to have met their deaths at Nero's hand including Peter, Paul, Aristarchus (Acts 19:29; Colossians 4:10), Carpus (2 Timothy 4:13), Epaphras (Colossians 1:7, 4:12; Philemon 1:23), Linus (2 Timothy 4:21), Prochorus (Acts 6:5), Silas (Acts 15:32, 17:15; 2 Corinthians 1:19; 1 Thessalonians 1:1; 2 Thessalonians 2:1; 1 Peter 5:12), and Trophimus (Acts 20:4, 21:29; 2 Timothy 4:20) who is alleged to have been beheaded alongside to Paul.[173]

Conclusion

At one time I was intrigued by the idea of Aquila as author, but my intrigue was replaced by reality. Others have elevated Priscilla above her husband and allowed their intrigue to overrule the facts. While they fit many of the criteria required of the author of Hebrews, they fail on several basic levels. First, there is no indication that Priscilla and Aquila had any relation to the recipient church which was probably in Israel. The author speaks with authority to them and it is doubtful that Priscilla and Aquila would have carried that authority in Israel, which is why Hoppin tries so desperately to claim that the recipients were in Ephesus. Second, and more important, is the fact that Priscilla and Aquila were most likely victims of Nero's persecution as most (albeit not all) traditions affirm. They would, therefore, have died before Hebrews was written. Third is the lack of any tradition whatsoever. Like Apollos in Alexandria, it would be odd for a figure so prominent in Rome to have left no tradition of his writing in the western church. Fourth is the lack of any positive evidence. It is not enough to suggest that they could have been the authors, but that there is evidence they were. This is a flaw with Apollos and it is no less a flaw here. Finally, if Priscilla and Aquila did write the epistle, which is doubtful, then the primary author was not Priscilla but Aquila for the epistle uses the masculine participle in Hebrews 11:32 which cannot be discarded or ignored.

Chart on Theory of Priscilla & Aquila's Authorship

Strengths	Neutral Arguments	Weaknesses
They were knowledgeable and learned in the Scriptures.	The multiple author argument is weak and tells us nothing.	Hebrews 11:32 uses a masculine participle negating Priscilla as the primary author.
They were of prominence in Rome.	It is unknown how much authority they would have had to speak to Israel.	They were most likely victims of Nero before the book of Hebrews was written.
They were close to the apostle Paul.		
They almost certainly knew Timothy.		
They were Jewish.		

As with Apollos and others they meet some of the criteria but there remain too many questions. The use of a masculine participle describing "I tell" positively negates Priscilla as the primary author, for her honesty eliminates the possibility of her deceiving her audience. The likelihood that they died under Nero elevates the probability that neither one wrote Hebrews.

Likelihood that Priscilla wrote Hebrews :
Nullified by Hebrews 11:32.

Likelihood that Aquila wrote Hebrews :
Doubtful.

Likelihood that Aquila and Priscilla wrote Hebrews :
Doubtful.

8

Suspect # 6 – Clement of Rome

Clement of Rome is variously considered the second or third overseer (bishop of Rome). Catholics, of course, count Peter which would make Clement either the third or forth bishop. His tenure has variously been dated. The ancient *Catalogus Liberianus* makes Clement overseer (or bishop) from 68 to 76 A.D.[174] while later Catholics, in order to accommodate Peter, have usually placed him much later, around 91 to 101 A.D.[175] Some even suggest he temporarily stepped down, thus held the office twice, or that his first term refer to a presbytership and the latter was as a bishop.[176]

If Clement is the same as that mentioned in Philippians 4:3 then we would think that the earlier date is more accurate,[177] although it is possible that he was but a young man when Philippians was written. On the other hand, internal evidence has led most to believe that the letter known as 1 Clement was written during the persecutions of Domitian in the 90s.[178] In either case, he eventually rose to become the overseer of the church of Rome amid the hostility of ancient Rome. His closeness to the apostle Paul and a member of Paul's circle of co-workers lend an air of authority to Clement which has served to make him one of the leading candidates for the author of Hebrews.[179]

The Clement Tradition
According to Eusebius (the early fourth century church historian) Origen, who lived in the third century, quoted a tradition (he does not say how old) that Clement may have had a hand in the writing of Hebrews.[180] Some believe that Clement was merely the translator of Hebrews, and not its author. In either case, the tradition, while is very old, does not seem to have been a prominent one. Aside from Origen's testimony of the tradition handed down to him there are no other extant citation of Clement in regard to Hebrews.

John Calvin, for one, favored that either Luke or Clement translated Paul,[181] but some have argued that the epistle of 1 Clement appears "definitely against the suggestion that Paul wrote Hebrews."[182] If so then this would speak against Clement translating Hebrews. In fairness, however, 1 Clement never mentions the book of Hebrews by name. It is obvious, however, that there are many quotations and paraphrases from Hebrews, but this itself is the controversy (see below), for was Clement truly quoting or alluding to Hebrews or was his style simply the same, being the author of both?

Regardless of which is true, I have already argued that Hebrews was probably not a translation. Had there been a need of a translation then Paul's command of the Greek language was such that "he would write a Greek letter without thought of employing a translator."[183] In fact, it is generally agreed that all of Paul's epistles were originally written by him in Greek. So again the question is why would Paul need a translator for Hebrews at all?

Perhaps Clement undertook on his own to translate Hebrews after Paul had already died? This would assume a Pauline authorship, which is in doubt. The real debate is whether or not Clement had any hand in writing Hebrews.

Clementine Style

The strongest argument made on behalf of Clement is that of the parallels between the epistle of 1 Clement and the book of Hebrews. Now while I cling to my earlier objection that arguments from "style" and vocabulary are overrated and overused, none doubt that Clement draws heavily from Hebrews. The question is whether or not Clement borrowed from the Scriptures or whether or not the similarities indicate a single author. The answer is not as simple as we might think.

Benjamin Bacon noted that "Clement has upwards of forty-seven echoes of Hebrews, and in chs. 9-18 of his epistle follows it seriatim."[184] Indeed, Clement lists of men of faith is virtually the exact same as Hebrews. The only difference is that Clement adds Lot's faith and omits Moses's. So close are the passages that Bacon said "in Clement's letter to the church of Corinth he often seems to be following [Hebrew's] argument point by point."[185] Nor is it a coincidence that Clement begins with the faith of Enoch, a man mentioned only once in the Old Testament (5:24) (aside from the genealogies), and ends with Rahab the prostitute, another character mentioned only briefly in the story of Joshua. On the other hand, it has been shown that James too uses Rahab as an illustration of faith,[186] so this is not to say that Enoch and Rahab are not great inspirations, but to eliminate any thinking that the "faith lists" in Hebrews and Clement are mere coincidences. *Clearly* Clement borrowed heavily from Hebrews.

Below is a chart highlighting some of the parallels between Hebrews 11 and 1 Clement 9-12. This is just a sampling. One might almost accuse Clement of plagiarism since he does not specifically say he is quoting from Hebrews.

Hebrew	1 Clement
"By faith Enoch was taken up so that he would not see death" (11:5).	"Let us set before us Enoch, who being found righteous in obedience was translated, and his death was not found" (9:3).
"By faith Noah, being warned *by God* about things not yet seen, in reverence prepared an ark for the salvation of his household, by which he condemned the world, and became an heir of the righteousness which is according to faith" (11:7).	"Noah, being found faithful, by his ministration preached regeneration unto the world, and through him the Master saved the living creatures that entered into the ark in concord" (9:4).
"By faith Abraham, when he was called, obeyed by going out to a place which he was to receive for an inheritance; and he went out, not knowing where he was going ..." (11:8-10)	"Abraham, who was called the 'friend,' was found faithful in that he rendered obedience unto the words of God. He through obedience went forth from his land and from his kindred and from his father's house, that leaving a scanty land and a feeble kindred and a mean house he might inherit the promises of God ..." (10:1-4).
"By faith Rahab the harlot did not perish along with those who were disobedient, after she had welcomed the spies in peace" (11:31).	"For her faith and hospitality Rahab the harlot was saved" (12:1-3)

This is but a small sampling. Any study of Clement makes it apparent that Clement was intimately familiar with the book of Hebrews, although he never refers to it by name. Now we cannot infer too much by his failure to quote Hebrews by name, for he also quotes Peter and even the gospels without stating as much. It is obviously Clement's style to quote anonymously. Nevertheless, this does beg the question as to Clement's relationship with Hebrews.

Although he does not propose that Clement wrote Hebrews, Edgar Goodspeed had said "that 1 Clement is so permeated with the literary influence of Hebrews becomes on this view of their relation more than ever natural and necessary. Something more than mere recentness is necessary to explain the great mass of reminiscence of Hebrews in 1 Clement, especially in Rome, where for nearly three centuries thereafter Hebrews is little noticed."[187]

Interestingly enough, whether we accept Clement's tenure as overseer from 68 to 76 A.D or from 91 to 101 A.D. bares impact upon this debate. If Clement was bishop from 91 to 101 A.D. it is more likely that he was merely quoting the sacred Scriptures and/or drawing inspiration from it. We could not conclude that they were written by the same person just because of the parallels.

Conversely, if he was overseer from 68 to 76 A.D. then, while we cannot by any means rule out that he was quoting Scripture, it becomes more plausible that he was author of both Hebrews and 1 Clement for he was certainly in Rome when Hebrews written. Of course, it could also mean that he was familiar with Hebrews even before it became accepted as canon of Scripture.

A Greek Epistle to Hebrews?
One of the most intriguing questions about Hebrews is why a letter to Hebrews, probably living in Israel, would have been written in Greek. Although some maintain that our copy is a translation from a lost Hebrew epistle, there is no tradition (as there is with Matthew's gospel) of a Hebrew original, nor do Greek scholars believe that the Greek found in Hebrews could be a translation unless the translator took many liberties with the original text (see my discussion in chapter two).

If this thesis is correct, then we would have to assume that the author did not know Hebrew. That would certainly fit very well with Clement, who is believed to be a gentile convert from Rome. Of course if true this is also one of Clement's biggest drawbacks for "what had he, who was a convert from among the Gentiles, to do with the churches of the Hebrews? What authority had he to *interpose* himself?"[188]

To this there are two answers. Firstly, some, and not just Catholics, argue that Clement believed he had such authority. Said Protestant church historian Philip Schaff, "it can hardly be denied that the document [1 Clement] reveals the sense of a certain superiority over all ordinary congregations."[189] While this is an overstatement, Clement's association with the Pauline circle certainly gave him an air of authority which appears at times in his epistle. It would not, therefore, be implausible to suggest that Clement would write a letter to a church in Israel. If he did, this would explain why the letter was written in Greek!

The second answer to this challenge is the fact that Clement may have been Jewish. Such prominent names as J.B. Lightfoot and Eberhard Nestle support his Jewish heritage.[190] Speculation that he was a "Hellenistic Jew"[191] is not new. Some have argued that 1 Clement's masterful use of Old Testament and Hebrew saints infers that he was a Jew.[192] Of course, the response is that he was influenced by the book of Hebrews, but even if this be true, it cannot be said with certainty whether Clement was or was not a Jew. We simply do not have enough information on Clement to make that determination.

Clement's Anonymous Epistle
Like Hebrews, 1 Clement nowhere mentions the name of its author. How then do we know that Clement even wrote 1 Clement? The answer, like that of the gospels and a few other epistles (1 John, 2 John, & 3 John), is found both within and without. For one thing, the recipients of the epistles knew who wrote the letters. While their names may not have appeared within the text of the letters, their name was carried either by the courier or by the seal of the letter, or in some other form. Technically, not even Hebrews was truly anonymous. Consequently, not all authors were in the habit of introducing themselves, as Paul and Peter did. 1 Clement is one of these. However, for this very reason there is debate as to whether or not the Clement of 1 Clement's epistle was truly the Clement of Philippians 4:3 or Flavius Clemens, the emperor Domitian's cousin and a former consul.[193]

In favor of Favius Clemens is the generally accepted date of 95 A.D. for the epistle. On the other hand, Clemens was executed by Domitian in 96 A.D. whereas the Clement who was bishop of Rome is presumed to have died in 101 A.D.[194] Moreover, Clemens and Clement should not be so easily confused. Although there may be an affinity for the two names, Rome had long accepted Clement as the bishop. This is also apparent in the text of 1 Clement where he takes a strong defense of bishops and presbyters (42:4-5, 44:1-4, 47:6, 54:2, and 57:1). Questions do remain as to Clement's tenure and death, but the attempt to attach Flavius Clemens name to 1 Clement is suspect. Tradition holds that Clement of Rome was that of Philippians 4:3, and given the prominence of Paul's companions it is logical to assume that Clement might well have risen to the overseer (or bishopry) of Rome following Paul's death. This seems not only logical, but probable.

As a result, the failure of Clement to sign his letters within the body of the text fits the style of Hebrews. The absence of a name is only relevant if the candidate was accustomed to signing his name within the text body. In this case we have clear evidence that Clement did not do so. This therefore fits his "style."

Other Evidence

In addition to these arguments we must ask how Clement fits in with the criteria determined in chapter two. The answer is surprisingly well, although not without difficulties.

In accordance with Hebrews 2:3 it a virtual certainty that Clement was a second generation Christian who heard the gospel from the apostles. Although it is conceivable that he was a Jew from Israel who knew Jesus in the beginning there is no evidence to support this. Most believe that he was a gentile or a Hellenistic Jew at best. In either case, it is not likely that he was among the first followers of Christ. If the traditional death date of 101 A.D. is accurate then it is almost certain that Clement was at best a young boy when Jesus walked in Jerusalem. He is therefore a second generation Christian taught by the apostles.

Among those apostles were Paul. He is called a "fellow worker" (Philippians 4:3) with Paul and would have been among his inner circle of friends and workers. This too fits the profile. It also strengthens the belief that he knew Timothy who was imprisoned in Rome under Nero.

Along with Timothy, Luke, and Mark, Clement appears to have been the only disciple mentioned in the Bible to have escaped death when living in Rome during Nero's persecution. His association with Rome also makes him a likely suspect, given that the epistle was most probably written from there (see Hebrews 13:24 and debate in chapter two).

Now there are some strong arguments against Clement as well. First, it is presumed that he was a gentile, although some doubt this (see above). Moreover, it is doubtful that he would have had the air of authority to speak to Jews in Israel (but see above). Finally, like Apollos there is little direct positive evidence that he wrote Hebrews. He is a good candidate with few weakness, but no real strengths.

Conclusion

When I began to write this book I found Clement to be an odd candidate. My personal inclination was to reject it out of hand, but as I began to examine him more closely I found him to be one of the strongest candidates. To be sure, we cannot say that Clement was the author, for there are too many questions which remain open. Nor can we say that the similarities between Hebrews and 1 Clement are not intentional on Clement's part. Nevertheless, Clement, like Apollos, is an intriguing candidate. He has few weaknesses, but equally few positive strengths. He fits most, but probably not all, the criteria required of the author, and yet nothing in the text can positively identify him as the author. Clement is therefore a fascinating possibility, but only a possibility.

Chart on Theory of Clementine Authorship

Strengths	Neutral Arguments	Weaknesses
He was a second generation Christian as Hebrews 2:3 suggests.	He may or may not have been a Jew.	Most believe that he was a gentile.
He was an overseer in Rome, from whence Hebrews appears to have been written.	His epistle is filled with allusions to Hebrews, but did he borrow those or was he the author?	He did not have authority to speak to Jews in Israel.
He was a member of Paul's "fellow workers" (Philippians 4:3)		
He almost certainly knew Timothy.		
He believed he had authority to speak to other churches.		
It was not his habit to sign his name.		
He probably didn't know Hebrew, hence he would write in Greek.		

Like Apollos, Clement seems to fit most of the criteria required and has only a few drawbacks, but like Apollos there is little solid evidence to connect him to Hebrews. The best evidence, being the dramatic similarities between 1 Clement and Hebrews, can be explained as inspiration rather than a common authorship and thus a neutral argument.

Likelihood that Clement wrote Hebrews :
Possible.

9

Suspect # 7 – Silas

Silas was a prophet (Acts 15:32) with whom Paul traveled in his second journey. He had been chosen by the apostles to accompany Paul along with a Judas Barsabbas (Acts 15:22). He is last heard of in Acts 18:5, indicating that he did not accompany Paul on his third missionary journey. However, he does appear in the epistles where 2 Corinthians 1:19 makes it clear that Silas and Silvanus are one and the same person (cf. Acts 17:15).[195] In addition to being a close associate of Paul he is called a "faithful brother" of Peter (1 Peter 5:12) and some say, his amenuensis or secretary.[196] Could he have written Hebrews?

Silas was a Jew and well respected in Jerusalem (Acts 15:32). As a companion of Paul he would have significant "Pauline" influences. He is also mentioned by Paul in both epistles to the Thessalonians, alongside with Timothy and Paul himself as a co-author (1 Thessalonians 1:1; 2 Thessalonians 2:1) thus it is clear that he knew Timothy and spoke with authority.

Despite these impressive credentials some say that Hebrews 2:3 eliminates Silas as Hebrew's author.[197] According to Acts 15:22 "it seemed good to the apostles and the elders, with the whole church, to choose men from among them to send to Antioch with Paul and Barnabas – Judas called Barsabbas, and Silas, leading men among the brethren." Now if Silas was a "leading man" among the church, we would assume that he had been among Jesus's followers in the beginning. Granted, this is assumption, but we know that Jesus appointed seventy disciples under the authority of the apostles (Luke 10:1) and it is a logical assumption that those chosen as "leading men among the brethren" were among the seventy. Although not a proven fact, it is logical.

There is also the universal silence of history in regard to Silas. Like Apollos there are no traditions of his authorship, which would be odd if indeed he had written the epistles. Nevertheless, the greater problem with Silas is the same which plagues many candidates; the date of his death. Like so many of the Biblical leaders who ventured to Rome (and many who did not), Silas is believed to have met his end during Nero's persecutions,[198] although there is small window during which he could have authored Hebrews.

Edward Armitage – The Christian Martyr – 1863

Too many mysteries remain concerning Silas. Although he fits some of the criteria required, there is no direct evidence at all to connect him to the book of Hebrews and no tradition to support it. Additionally, he was probably a follower of Christ from the beginning, which would eliminate him as a valid candidate. Moreover, accounts of his martyrdom make it suspect as to whether he was still alive when Hebrews was written.

Chart on Theory of Silas Authorship

Strengths	Neutral Arguments	Weaknesses
He was Jewish.	He is listed as a co-author of the Thessalonian epistles.	He was probably not a second generation Christian (cf. Acts 15:22)
He was a close associate of Paul.		He probably died during Nero's persecution.
He knew Timothy personally.		There is no tradition of a Silas authorship.
He was well respected in Jerusalem.		

Silas is conjecture. He is one of many Biblical names who could have written Hebrews, but there is no real evidence to support that thesis and some convincing evidence against it.

Likelihood that Silas wrote Hebrews :
Improbable, but possible.

10

Suspect # 8 – Mark

As I have stated, there are but four Biblical leaders known to have been in Rome during Nero's persecution who escaped with their life. Mark is one of those ... or is he? The traditions of Mark are divided and many do indeed believe that he died during Nero's persecution while other maintain that he survived and returned to the church of Alexandria which he is credited with having founded.[199] If Mark survived Nero's brutal persecution he remains one of three viable candidates, but is he a good candidate?

Let us start with Mark's death. The *Babylon Namebook* says that he died in the eight year of Nero, but the church father Dorotheus places his death in the times of Trajan (between 112 and 117 A.D.).[200] Upon close examination, the early date must be rejected, for the eighth year of Nero would 62 A.D. when we know Mark was alive and with Peter and Paul in Rome (cf. 2 Timothy 4:11; Philemon 1:24; 1 Peter 5:13), neither of whom died that year. Additionally, Eusebius claimed that Mark served as the bishop of the church in Alexandria.[201] In *Apostles After Jesus* I argued that the date for this bishopry would be approximately 70 to 80 A.D.[202] If this is true then Mark of Alexandria died under Trajan, not Nero. Finally, all ancient traditions, even those which claim Mark died under Nero, place the location of his death in Egypt! This suggest that the date, rather than the location, is in error.

Assuming Mark did survive Nero's persecution he would have been alive to have written Hebrews, but does he fit the criteria? Certainly Mark was in Rome (Colossians 4:10; Philemon 24) around the time Hebrews was written, but some argue he was never a member of Paul's "inner circle" on account of their dispute in Acts (cf. Acts 15:37-40),[203] but this is a bad argument for they were certainly reconciled by the time of Paul's imprisonment (2 Timothy 4:11) and appeared to be close in several of Paul's letters where he is called a "fellow worker" (Philemon 1:24) and "useful to me in service" (Colossians 4:10). So it would appear that Mark was "Pauline" and knew Timothy.

Another argument in his favor is that his youth (if tradition is to be believed) infers that he was probably not an eyewitness to Jesus. Traditions also state that Mark wrote his gospel under the supervision of Peter since Mark was not present.[204] This would fit Hebrews 2:3, making Mark a second generation believer.

One final support for Mark is presumably his connection to the Alexandrian church. This could explain the constant use of the *Septuagint* as well as the preference for Greek. Of course by the same token, if Mark, who is revered in Alexandria, was the author of Hebrews we would ask why no eastern tradition names him the author. In this respect, he has the same flaw as Apollos, another candidate from Alexandria.

If these evidences support Mark's authorship then "style" is a definite mark against Mark. While I have admitted to my distaste for the "style" arguments I must admit that it is hard to imagine Hebrews having been written by the same hand as Mark. John Ebrard believes that Mark's "style" is decidedly different from Hebrews,[205] and I must agree. Lenski, less charitably, stated that Mark's "Greek is inferior to that of Matthew."[206] Since Hebrews is often considered best and most eloquent of Greek in the Bible, this would speak against a Markan authorship.

In short, Mark is one of four Biblical leaders in Rome during the great persecution who is known to have survived. He fits most of the criteria but has no direct evidence to support him. His "style" in the gospel is very different from Hebrews, and while the subject matter is different (one is a history, the other a polemic discourse), it is hard to imagine the same author wrote both.

Chart on Theory of Markan Authorship

Strengths	Neutral Arguments	Weaknesses
He was well respected in the Christian community as the author of one of the gospels.	His "style" is marketably different from Hebrews.	There is no tradition of a Markan authorship.
He was a close associate of Paul.		
He knew Timothy personally.		
He was Jewish.		
His connection to Alexandria would explain his use of Greek and the *Septuagint*.		
He may have been in Rome when Hebrews was written.		

Few weaknesses does not equal strength. Mark fits many of the criteria and has few drawbacks, but he again lacks any solid evidence, or even tradition, that would connect him to the book of Hebrews. Although I have considered arguments from style to be weak, I admit that I find it hard to believe that Hebrews was written by the same person as Mark's gospel.

Likelihood that Silas wrote Hebrews :
Possible.

11

Other "Suspects"

Along with the aforementioned candidates countless other names have been bandied about. Some are more credible than others. For example, Sixtus Semens claimed that Tertullian wrote Hebrews,[207] but Tertullian himself attributed Hebrews to Barnabas, for when he quotes "the epistle of Barnabas" we find that the quotation is actually from Hebrews 6:4-6.[208] Hence, Tertullian quotes Hebrews second hand, identifying it as that of Barnabas. Yet another author even mentioned Stephen (Acts 6:5–8:2) as a possible author![209]

    Seven candidates remain. I have listed these candidates here (in alphabetical order) in a single chapter, not because they are weaker *per se* than the previous candidates, but simply because there is less evidence. Without a great deal of evidence, there is no reason to devote a single chapter to each man. One of them may well be proven to be the author of Hebrews in eternity but for now I can only list the evidence which I have found before me. Let the reader be his own judge.

Aristion
Some have proposed that Aristion was the author of Hebrews.[210] The first question is, "who is Aristion?" Aristion, although not mentioned in the Bible, is said by Papias (a disciple of the apostle John) to have been "the Lord's disciple."[211] Some traditions make him

one of the seventy disciples of Luke 10:1,[212] and one medieval author suggested that he was the author of Mark 16:9-20.[213] Traditions vary, placing his martyrdom in Salamis, Greece or even Alexandria, Egypt[214] but the later is probably confused with a later Aristion who was a bishop of "lesser Alexandria" in Cilicia.[215] In any case, he could not be the author of Hebrews for if he was a follower of Christ from the beginning then he could almost certainly not have penned Hebrews 2:3.

Chart on Theory of Aristion's Authorship

Strengths	Neutral Arguments	Weaknesses
He was well respected in the Christian community as "the Lord's disciple."	Almost nothing is known about Aristion except that he apparently was one of the seventy (Luke 10:1)	He was an original follower of Christ and thus negated by Hebrews 2:3.
He was Jewish.	.	He does not appear to have any connection to Rome.

Almost nothing is known of Aristion. This fact does not negate him, but the fact that he is a first generation follower of Christ probably does. He is thus very unlikely.

Likelihood that Aristion wrote Hebrews :
Highly unlikely.

Epaphras
Epaphras is another Pauline associate whose name has been bandied about in recent times, although not with regularity.[216] Like Aristion almost nothing is known about him except for his mention by Paul in three passages. He is mentioned twice in Colossians (Colossians 1:7; 4:12) and once in Philemon as a "fellow prisoner" (Philemon 1:23). According to

ancient martyrologies he even "shared the same dungeon with Paul."[217] Of course these same martyrologies place Epaphras's death at the same time as Paul,[218] so if Paul had died before Hebrews was written, then so had Epaphras. The evidence in his favor is simply that he was an associate of Paul and Timothy who was in Rome close to the time Hebrews was written. Nothing else can be said for or against Epaphras.

Chart on Theory of Epaphras' Authorship

Strengths	Neutral Arguments	Weaknesses
He was a close associate of Paul.		He was probably dead before Hebrews was written.
He knew Timothy.		

Little evidence exist and little is needed for if he was executed alongside Paul then he was probably dead before Hebrews was written.

Likelihood that Epaphras wrote Hebrews :
Unlikely.

Jude
Another name which has recurred in modern times is that of Jude.[219] Many have immediately dismissed Jude based on Hebrews 2:3, for if he was the step-brother of Jesus, as many argue,[220] than it would make no sense for him to have said, "after it was at the first spoken through the Lord, it was confirmed to us by those who heard" (2:3) as if he had not been present.[221]

Now this argument seems enough to dismiss Jude, but only if we can concur with the assumption that he was Jesus' step-brother or half-brother. To this end we must investigate both James and Jude to determine who they were and what relationship they had to the Lord.

Who Was James?

Jude was the brother of James (Jude 1:1), but which James? In order to identify Jude, we must first identify James.

James the son of Alphæus (Matthew 10:3; March 3:18; Acts 1:13) is generally believed to be James the Less (March 15:40) but there is another James called the Just in history. This begs the question. Were there two James? Was James the Less the same as James the Just? If not, was James the Just the one of which Acts speaks so prominently? Interestingly enough, many believe so. The primary reason for this revolves around whether or not James was a step-brother, half-brother, or cousin of Jesus. Since John 7:5 declares that Jesus's brothers were not believers many Protestants reject the idea that James the Less was Jesus's step-brother. Consequently, they believe that James the Just was a convert after the Resurrection of Jesus.[222] Is this so? The first step in determining James's relationship to Jesus is to examine all the critical passages side by side.

Matthew	Mark	Luke	John
"Among them was Mary Magdalene, and Mary the mother of James and Joseph, and the mother of the sons of Zebedee." (Matthew 27:56)	"Among whom were Mary Magdalene, and Mary the mother of James the Less and Joses, and Salome." (Mark 15:40)	"Now they were Mary Magdalene and Joanna and Mary the *mother* of James; also the other women with them" (Luke 24:10)	"Standing by the cross of Jesus were His mother, and His mother's sister, Mary the *wife* of Clopas, and Mary Magdalene." (John 19:25)

So the only appearance of the name James the Less is Mark 15:40. A few passages later it reappears in Mark 6:1-3 where Jesus's critics say, "Is not this the carpenter, the son of Mary, and brother of James and Joses and Judas and Simon? Are not His sisters here with us?" So it is clear that James the Less was the son of a Mary who had brothers named Joseph, Judas (Jude), and Simon. Was this Mary, the mother of Jesus?

Matthew 27:55 explicitly states that "many women were there" (Matthew 27:55) at the cross. This includes Jesus's mother Mary, Mary Magdalene, Salome, Joanna, and Mary the wife of Clopas (or Cleophas). So there were at least three Marys present. The question is, which one is the mother of James, Joseph, Judas, and Simon? Matthew 13:55-56 and Mark 6:3 appear to make clear that these are indeed the step-brothers of Jesus, but there is a problem with this.

The apostle James is called James the son of Alphæus (Matthew 10:3; March 3:18; Acts 1:13). Hence it seems apparent that the apostle James the Less is not James the Just, but the James of Mark 15:40 is explicitly called "the Less" and is the same as that of Matthew 13:55-56 and Mark 6:3! How can this confusion be resolved? Who is Alphæus?

In *Apostles After Jesus* I discuss this debate in some detail. Here I will offer a shortened version. There are four possible solutions to this dilemma.

One view is that James was Jesus's half-brother by another wife.[223] The problem with this view is that it assumes Joseph was as much as thirty years Mary's senior and also fails to explain the term "son of Alphæus" since Joseph had no ancestor by that name.

The second view is that James was Jesus's cousin, the son of Mary's natural sister.[224] The term "brothers" is then generic for both Jesus's immediate family *and* His extended family, which would include cousins. The problem with this argument is the absurdity of having two sisters with the same name.

A third view also makes James the cousin of Jesus by Mary's step-sister, also called Mary. In this case Mary, the wife of Cleophas, is Joseph's sister, but this fails to explain the "son of Alphæus." Some suggest that James was the son by a previous marriage but this is idle speculation.

A fourth view is similar to the third, accepting that James is the cousin of Jesus by Joseph's sister, but differs in that it argues that Cleophas and Alphæus are different Hellenizations of the same Hebrew names.[225] The argument is technical, and I will not repeat it here, but John Gill, the nineteenth century Calvinist, presented a long defense of this view in his commentary which I am inclined to accept with reservations.[226]

So we can conclude that the James Alphæus was James the Less and a cousin of Jesus, who was a part of the extended family present when Jesus's critics referred to his "brothers and sisters." It is true that Jesus did have step-brothers and sisters through Mary and Joseph, a fact even Saint Jerome accepted, but James is not one of those. He is the son of Mary Cleophas, or Alphæus.

One piece of the puzzle remains. What of this James the Just? Was this James found in the book of

Acts the step-brother of Jesus or the cousin and apostle known as James the Less? Galatians 1:19 would seem to answer that question for Paul appears to call the apostle James by the title, "James, the Lord's brother." This makes them one and the same![227]

Who Was Jude?

Now we must ask, "who was Jude?" The epistle of Jude is signed, "Jude ... brother of James" (v. 1) but says nothing more of his relationship. Like James there is a debate as to Jude's relationship with Jesus. Was he the apostle known as Judas Lebbæus, surnamed Thaddæus? Jude 17 seems to eliminate that possibility for it says, "you, beloved, ought to remember the words that were spoken beforehand by the apostles of our Lord Jesus Christ." This implies that Jude was not one of "the apostles of our Lord Jesus Christ," and therefore not Judas Thaddæus.

So Jude, the brother of James, was a cousin of Jesus by Joseph's sister, also named Mary. He was among the apostles but was well known and revered in the Christian community as a leader of the church. If tradition is to be believed than Jude was also a bishop at Jerusalem, for Eusebius makes him the last bishop of Jerusalem,[228] although there are question marks revolving around Eusebius' claims.[229] One thing which does seem apparent, however, is that Jude served in Jerusalem until he was driven out shortly before the siege of Jerusalem. Of no small importance is the fact that Jude would have left Jerusalem at the same time that James the Just was martyred on the Temple mount; the same James who was Jude's brother!

The Evidence

Several key points have been made. First, Jude was the brother of James the Just and a member of Jesus's extended family. He was well respected in the Jewish community and would have been a perfect authority figure for Jewish Christians who had left Jerusalem, as Jude had.

Another important fact is the similarities in the epistle of Jude and Hebrews. Both mention Enoch and it is said that the typology of Hebrews matches very well is the style and appeal of Jude. There is also parallel between Hebrews and Jude's appeal to remember those who had come before them (cf. Hebrews 10:32 and Jude 17). Although the epistle of Jude is very short, too short for a fair comparison, there are indeed similarities of style and substance.

All this seems to make Jude an appealing candidate but there are a number of issues against him. First, if he had left Jerusalem shortly before the siege then we would ask how he got to Rome and why he would chastise them for their spiritual immaturity (Hebrews 5:12-14) if he was a part of that church. Moreover, there is no tradition or evidence that Jude ever went to Rome. The best evidence has him dying at a ripe old age in Beruit, Lebanon.[230] Finally, Hebrews 2:3 again seems to negate Jude, for if he was a cousin of Jesus and a brother of the apostle James then it would hard to picture him saying those words.

Conclusion

Jude is the most intriguing of these last candidates, but intrigue does not make truth. Jude probably never went to Italy and was more likely be among the recipients of the epistle than its author. Furthermore, as a relative of Jesus he is nullified by Hebrews 2:3.

Chart on Theory of Jude's Authorship

Strengths	Neutral Arguments	Weaknesses
He was a leader in the Christian community in Jerusalem.	He had probably fled Jerusalem shortly before Hebrews was written.	Hebrews 2:3 appears to negate any relative of Jesus.
He uses imagery reminiscent of Hebrews.		He does not appear to have any connection to Rome.
He was Jewish.		

Jude is intriguing because of his relationship to the church in Jerusalem and because similarities in Hebrews and Jude, but his closeness to Jesus and the likelihood that he never traveled to Italy negate his being a good candidate.

Likelihood that Jude wrote Hebrews :
Unlikely, but possible.

Peter

Peter has never been one of the more popular choices, and with good reason, but he has been named as a candidate by some in the past.[231] As a presumed leader of the Roman church, he would certainly fit with Hebrews 13:24, but the evidence goes downhill from here.

It is said that Hebrews was written to the same recipients as 1 Peter (1:1),[232] but this is conjecture on too many levels. Some even doubt that the "aliens" of 1 Peter 1:1 are properly Jews, saying instead that all believers are "aliens" living in a strange world (cf. Ephesians 2:19; Hebrews 11:13). However, assuming that the 1 Peter was written to the Jews of Asia Minor, which is probably true, the evidence does not support that Hebrews was written to this same audience. In chapter two the evidence for the recipients was laid out, so the reader may judge for himself.

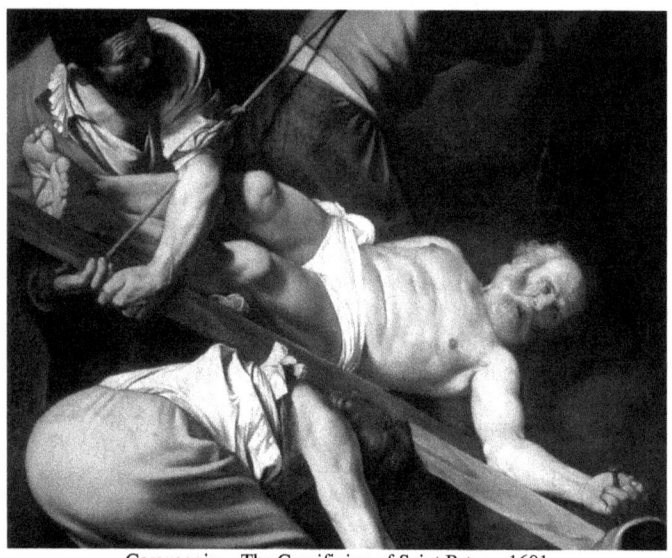
Caravaggio – The Crucifixion of Saint Peter – 1601

Aside from the application of Hebrews 2:3, which has negated so many candidates, the Peter thesis has many other problems. To begin with there is "no historical record of any church tradition" that attributes Hebrews to Peter.[233] Moreover, like Paul, Peter was accustomed to signing his epistles, which would make Hebrews an anomaly if he had indeed written it. The greatest problem is, again, with the date of his death. Although historians vary on the exact date, there is no question that Peter died either early during Nero's persecutions or in the middle. The early date, which I maintain, is 65 A.D.[234] The latest date is 67 A.D. Both are before Hebrews appears to have been written.

Chart on Theory of Petrine Authorship

Strengths	Neutral Arguments	Weaknesses
He was among the most respected leaders in the Christian community.		He was an apostle and thus negated by Hebrews 2:3.
He was Jewish, and ministered to the Jewish communities.		He almost assuredly had died before Hebrews was written.
He was in Rome in the 60s.		There is no tradition of Peter having written Hebrews.
		Peter was in the habit of signing his epistles.

Very little evidence supports Peter. This is conjecture nullified by the majority of evidence.

Likelihood that Peter wrote Hebrews :
Virtually impossible.

Philip the Evangelist
Another rare candidate sometimes mentioned is that of Philip the Evangelist.[235] Like Jude, the first thing which must be determined is whether or not Philip the Evangelist was the same as Philip the apostle.

Much Catholic tradition holds that Philip the apostle was one and the same as Philip the Evangelist. However, there is good reason to reject this. According to Acts 6:2-5:

"The twelve summoned the congregation of the disciples and said, 'It is not desirable for us to neglect the word of God in order to serve tables. Therefore, brethren, select from among you seven men of good reputation, full of the Spirit and of wisdom, whom we may put in charge of this task.' But we will devote ourselves to prayer and to the ministry of the word. The statement found approval with the whole congregation ; and they chose Stephen, a man full of faith and of the Holy Spirit, and Philip, Prochorus, Nicanor, Timon, Parmenas and Nicolas, a proselyte from Antioch."

So we see that Philip the Evangelist was one of the seven deacons appointed by the apostles. It would at first then appear that the two are different Philips, but some argue that "the Twelve complained that administrative concerns were causing them to neglect the preaching of God's word, and thus they appointed the deacons to assist them ... since the college of deacons serve the Hellenistic wing of the Church, it was conceivable that the Twelve felt that one of their number should be a part of that body."[236] This seems logical, except when we read of this same Philip in Acts 21:8-9. There is it said that Paul entered "the house of Philip the evangelist, who was one of the seven" who had "four virgin daughters who were prophetesses." Why would one of the *twelve* be identified as "one of the seven"? Surely this must be a different Philip from the apostle or else he would not be designated as "one of the seven" (Acts 21:9), but one of "the Twelve" (Acts 6:2).

In addition to this Biblical evidence, there is evidence from history as well, for Clement of Alexandria said that "Philip gave his daughters [plural] in marriage,"[237] but Polycrates said that of the four virgin daughters, all but one died a virgin.[238] This is only reconcilable if there were two Philips. The apostle can easily be rejected as the author based not only on Hebrews 2:3 but also the fact that he was probably the second apostle to die a martyr's death, having been stoned to death in northern Africa in the 50s.[239]

This leaves us with Philip the Evangelist who is alleged to have lived into the second century.[240] On his behalf it can be said that he was a Jew and probably very eloquent and persuasive preacher. He must have at least known Paul (Acts 21:8-9) although it cannot be said how close he was to Paul. Additionally, as a member of the seven deacons he would be well respected in Jerusalem and the Jewish church. Unfortunately, the support ends here. Owing to his election as one of the seven deacons only a short time after Pentecost it is almost certain that he was a follower of Christ during His ministry, and thus eliminated by Hebrews 2:3. Furthermore, there is no evidence that he ever went to Rome. And finally, there is not tradition of any kind to lend credibility to it. We have no information on Philip's knowledge of Greek and no reason to know why he would have used the *Septuagint* so much if he had. In short, we have no evidence. Philip is idle speculation, and not the best speculation. He must be categorized as another unlikely suspect.

Chart on Theory of Philip's Authorship

Strengths	Neutral Arguments	Weaknesses
As one of the seven deacons he would be respected in Jerusalem.	We have no knowledge of his Greek prowess or knowledge.	He was probably a first generation Christian (cf. Hebrews 2:3.)
He was a persuasive speaker.		There is no evidence he ever went to Rome.
He was Jewish.		No tradition exist to support this notion.

There is little evidence on behalf of Philip, but little against him either. The main drawback is that he was probably a follower of Christ before the resurrection and thus negated by Hebrews 2:3.

Likelihood that Philip wrote Hebrews :
Highly unlikely.

Timothy

This seems a rather odd suggestion given that he is mentioned in the third person in the epistle (13:23)! However, the subscription found in the King James Bible has led some to believe that Timothy may have at least been a joint author. Certainly Timothy fits much of the criteria. He was a second generation Christian and obviously a close acquaintance of Paul. Most interesting is that his father was a Greek, but his mother was Jewish (Hebrews 16:1). This mixed heritage would explain the heavy reliance upon the *Septuagint* and Greek while at the same time explaining the strong Jewish flavor of the epistle!

All of this sounds very convincing, except that the entire passage of Hebrews 13:23 seems to eliminate Timothy from serious consideration. It reads, "Take notice that our brother Timothy has been released, with whom, if he comes soon, I will see you." So "he" cannot be "I," the author.

Nevertheless, there is a curious postscript found in the majority text and the older King James versions. It says, "Written to the Hebrews from Italy, by Timothy." What could this mean? Was Timothy a co-author? Perhaps Timothy was the secretary? Is this a bad translation? Is the postscript even original, for it does not even appear in the New King James Bible!

There are two issues regarding the postscript. The first is the translation. The second is its genuineness. In regard to the translation, "by Timothy" is rendered "sent by Timotheus" in the old Geneva Bible. This is obviously what is meant. The Greek word for "by" used here is δια (*dia*) which most naturally means "through, by means of, with."[241] "Through" is the best meaning here, although the possibility of "with" is doubtless what intrigues advocates of Timothy, for this could imply co-authorship.

Why then is the postscript absent even from the New King James Bible? Like the title of the epistles, which does not appear on the original letters, scribes would add the title for reference. So also scribes would sometimes add postscripts for themselves. Such postscripts are not intended to be taken as a part of the original manuscript, but on rare occasions they may be so mistaken. Here is an example where there are many ancient variants.

The oldest manuscripts contain no postscript, ending only with the words, "Grace be with you all." So it is with the most ancient Papyrus 46 ($\mathfrak{P}^{46}$). However, some ancient codices do contain variants of the postscript. The Codex Sinaiticus (ℵ) and

Ephraemi (C) add "to the Hebrews." The Alexandrinus (A) adds "to the Hebrews written from Rome." Nonetheless, the first manuscript to contain variants of "by Timothy" is the ninth century Codex Mosquensis (K) followed by the *Textus Receptus*, or Majority text (𝔐), passed down through the church.[242]

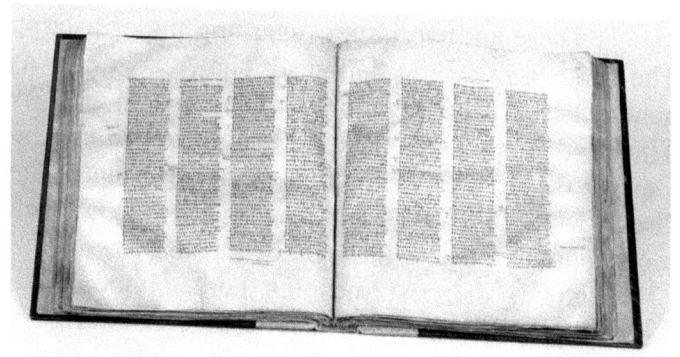

The Codex Sinaiticus

Obviously, the postscripts found in the *Textus Receptus* were scribal notes and not a part of the original text. It reflects tradition, which is of some support in Timothy's cause, but the problem with Timothy being a co-author is the fact that the author states unequivocally, "*if* he comes" (13:23). Since Timothy had just been released from prison, it seems that the author and Timothy had not seen each other recently. The author himself is not sure *if* Timothy will be able to come or not.

The biggest problem is that even if Timothy were a co-author, which is doubtful, he was not its primary author. Consequently, we are still left with the same fundamental question we had at the beginning. Who wrote Hebrews?

Chart on Theory of Timothean Authorship

Strengths	Neutral Arguments	Weaknesses
He was well respected in the Christian community.	The postscript does not prove that Timothy had a hand in the writing.	He is mentioned in the third person, and thus could not be the author.
He was half Jewish, with a Greek father (Hebrews 16:1).		Timothy does not appear to have been present when the letter was written (13:23).
His mixed parentage explains the use of Greek.		
He was a very close companion of Paul.		
He was a second generation Christian.		

Despite some surprising strengths, its obvious flaw is that Timothy is clearly not its primary author, as seen in Hebrews 13:23. Even his co-authorship is questionable, to say the least.

Likelihood that Timothy wrote Hebrews :
Unlikely as co-author. Impossible as primary author.

Titus

Our last candidate is Titus, to whom Paul wrote one of his epistles. He was a close associate of the apostle, whom is called "my true child in a common faith" (Titus 1:4), and he probably knew Timothy as well. We also know that he could read and write Greek because he was a gentile. Or was he? Here is a dilemma. If he was a gentile then he almost certainly did not write Hebrews. Some, however, argue he was half Jewish.

It is said by some that "Titus's Jewish heritage, if known to the Galatians, would explain the 'not even' (ουδε) in Gal. 2:3. We could then paraphrase: 'Not even Titus (whom you know had Jewish heritage) ... was compelled to be circumcised.'"[243] Thus it is argued that Paul, in debating circumcision, would not have mentioned Titus if he had not had Jewish blood. Nonetheless, this argument falls apart for several reasons.

If Titus's father was Jewish then he would be considered a Jew regardless of whether the mother was a Jew or not. He would then have been circumcised in childhood as per Jewish law and custom. If, however, his mother was Jewish, but not his father, then he would not have been considered Jewish in antiquity at all. Even though today Jews are reckoned by the mother, in the time of Titus only the father was reckoned.

The most critical problem with this speculation is the context of Galatians 2:3. It says, "not even Titus, who was with me, though he was a Greek, was compelled to be circumcised" (Galatians 2:3). Note that the "not even" is connected to his being with Paul and being known to the Galatians. There is nothing to hint at Jewish heritage, for Paul explicitly says, "he was a Greek." Greek means gentiles. It can mean nothing else.

Since Titus was gentile, he could almost certainly not have written Hebrews.[244] There is no real evidence to support Titus and Galatians 2:3 speaks strongly against Titus. Like many of Paul's companions he has become one of a long list of candidates selected from idle speculation rather than from actual evidence.

Chart on Theory of Titus's Authorship

Strengths	Neutral Arguments	Weaknesses
He was a close companion of Paul.		He was a gentile (cf. Galatians 2:3)
He probably knew Timothy.		There is no tradition of Titus as author.
He knew Greek.		

Titus is idle speculation with little support. The fact that he was a gentile (Galatians 2:3) weighs heavily against his being the author of Hebrews.

Likelihood that Titus wrote Hebrews :
Extremely unlikely.

Summary

Of these final candidates few can be taken seriously. The theory of Timothy's co-authorship is curiously intriguing, but wrong. Jude seems the strongest candidate from among this crowd, but his relationship to the Lord seems to negate his being the author based on Hebrews 2:3.

Doubtless many other Biblical names could be tossed around. Without evidence, they would all be idle speculation. Perhaps the fact that there are so many names tossed around is simply a reflection of how weak the evidence is for other authors. If the evidence strongly supported other candidates, there would be no need for such speculations.

12

Conclusion

The world loves a mystery. We love unsolved mysteries the most. Of course, this is the irony, for the reason we like unsolved mysteries is so that we can try to "solve" the mystery ourselves. Truly the author of Hebrews is a mystery.

If we have a mystery, then let us attempt to solve it as a detective would do. Let us take Sherlock Holmes's thesis that "if we eliminate the impossible, whatever is left, however unlikely, must be the truth."[245] Thus we should work in reverse. Remembering our original criteria, let us one by one begin to eliminate the suspects.

Because he spoke as one with authority we assume that he was a person mentioned in the New Testament. This assumption may be just that; assumption. Nevertheless, if we take this for granted, then our suspect list begins with the names of all those found in the New Testament. Now based on Hebrews 2:3 the author was almost certainly not an apostle, nor one of the seventy (Luke 10:1), nor one of the seven deacons (Acts 6:2-5), for he appears to have been a second generation believer. This also eliminates anyone who was a follower in the gospels. Unfortunately, this still leaves us with countless suggestions. Bear in mind that there are countless disciples mentioned in the Bible of whom we know nothing. In Romans alone Paul mentions by name thirty-five different colleagues in Romans 16 alone!

Candidate	Criteria #1	#2	#3	#4	#5	#6	#7
Apollos	Yes	Unknown	Probably	Yes	Yes	Yes	Yes
Aristion	Yes	Unknown	Unknown	No	Unknown	Unknown	Yes
Barnabas	Yes	No	Probably	Unknown	Yes	Yes	Yes
Clement of Rome	No (?)	Yes	Yes	Yes (?)	Yes	Yes (?)	Yes (?)
Epaphras	Unknown	No (?)	Unknown	Yes (?)	Unknown	Yes	Unknown
Jude	Yes	Yes	Unknown	No	Yes	Yes (?)	Yes
Luke	No (?)	Yes	Yes	Yes	Yes	Yes	Yes
Mark	Yes	Yes	Yes	Yes	Yes	Yes	Yes
Paul	Yes	No	Yes	No	Yes	Yes	Yes
Peter	Yes	No	Yes	No	Yes	Yes	Yes
Philip the Evangelist	Yes	Yes	Unknown	No	Yes	Yes (?)	Yes (?)
Priscilla and Aquila	Yes	No (?)	Probably	Yes	Yes	Yes	Yes
Silas	Yes	No (?)	Unknown	No (?)	Probably	Yes	Yes
Timothy	Yes	Yes	Yes	Yes	Probably	Yes	Yes
Titus	Yes	Yes	Yes	Yes (?)	Probably	Yes (?)	Yes

Legend : 1. Was he Jewish? 2. Was he alive in 68 or 69 A.D.? 3. Was he fluent in Greek? 4. Was he a 2nd generation Christian? 5. Was he an eloquent speaker/writer? 6. Did he know Timothy? 7. Did he have authority in the Israel?

When we match all of the popular candidates passed down through the ages with the original criteria we find that we can then safely eliminate virtually all of them! Could one of these criteria be in error? Certainly, or perhaps Luke and/or Clement were not gentiles after all? This is another possibility. If we leave room for such possible errors, and as well we should, we have a list of possibilities, but only possibilities. Below is a summary of my own conclusions.

Candidate	**Probability Factor**
Clement of Rome	Possible
Mark	Possible
Apollos	Possible, but unknown
Luke	Possible, but not likely
Silas	Improbable, but possible
Aquila	Doubtful
Aquila and Priscilla	Doubtful
Paul	Doubtful, but possible
Barnabas	Highly doubtful
Jude	Unlikely, but possible
Timothy as co-author	Unlikely
Epaphras	Unlikely
Philip the Evangelist	Highly unlikely
Aristion	Highly unlikely
Titus	Extremely unlikely
Peter	Virtually impossible
Priscilla	Impossible
Timothy as sole author	Impossible

The reader should note that when I began my investigation Barnabas was my favorite candidate and Clement was among my least favorite candidates. Having examined the possibilities Clement now ranks at the top, although by no means is his authorship a certainty, and Barnabas now appears a remote possibility. Thus, the facts do not always lend themselves to personal favorites or biases.

I have attempted to lay out the evidences for and against all of the major candidates. The reader may decide for himself whether I have made a fair evaluation. Nevertheless, my own conclusion is the same that of Origen who famously said, "who wrote the epistle, in truth God alone knows."[246]

Appendix

Hebrews in the Canon

Some so-called liberal theologians and Bible critics claim that the Biblical canon (the list of inspired authoritative books of the Bible) developed over many centuries with no unified agreement. This urban myth is promoted in many liberal seminaries and schools by an easy sleight of hand. This is usually done by ignoring the fact that "books" as we know them today did not exist until close the time of Constantine (hence the Constantinian conspiracy theories). Instead, they had scrolls. Obviously a person's library might have included Biblical scrolls and non-Biblical scrolls, but which were inspired and which were not? This is where the critic can play games, and nowhere more so than with Hebrews.

Since no one is even sure who actually wrote Hebrews, it is not a surprise that its place in the canon has been questions by some. Certainly there was those in antiquity who may not have accepted it, just as there are some who reject it today. Just as we have Mormons who add the Book of Mormon to the Bible, there were cults that added books the Bible, and there were cults which rejected some of the Biblical canon. So how can we decide what the canon of the Bible truly was, and whether or not Hebrews was a part of that canon? When was it accepted as sacred Scripture? Since I address the question of the larger canon in the appendices to *Controversies in the Gospels* and *Controversies in the Acts and Epistles*, I will predominantly restrict my debate here to Hebrews.

Nevertheless, the first question is when and how the canon came to be formed at all. One thing is certain. Contrary to popular myth "the Council of Nicea did not address the issue of canonicity"[247] for that issue had long been settled. Although it hard to prove an exact "date" at which the canon was accepted, it is clear that most believers followed the same books, with a few possible exceptions, very early on. The four gospels, for example, are consistently quoted and cited as Scripture by all the early church fathers, as are most of the Pauline epistles. Despite this, some evangelical authors blindly follow the argument that if a church father quoted from an apocryphal book then he must have accepted it as canon as well.[248] This argument is pure assumption. Nowhere can it be proven that quoting a book makes it sacred canon anymore than my quotations from secular authors. How then can we know when they were quoting Scripture and when they were quoting secular books?

There are several ways in which we can determine whether an author held a book to be sacred canon. One is the introduction of a passage using certain phrases, such as "it is written." This phrase, and similar ones, was a common way of introducing a sacred passage. In some cases they will actually say, "the Scripture says." There is yet another way. As early as the second century we have an actual list of the canonical books. The Muratorian canon unearthed in the nineteenth century demonstrated that the canon had most likely been accepted at least by the time of its composition, dated around 170 A.D.[249] Although there are some peculiarities surrounding the list, its discovery shot holes in the liberal thesis that there was no such things a Biblical canon in the early church. What peculiarities? The main attack is the fact that

Since I am restricting my discussion to the book of Hebrews, James, 1 and 2 Peter, and 3 John appear to be omitted.[250] I say "appear" because the document is fragmentary, having been damaged over the centuries, hence some have argued that they missing books *could* have been listed.[251] In any case, it is true that some books may not have been universally accepted until close to the end of the second century. Hebrews may be one of those. Why?

First, Hebrews was one of the last books of the New Testament to be written. Most of the New Testament was written in the 50s and 60s. Hebrews was written shortly before 70 A.D. and Revelation in the 90s. It is little wonder that these two books were among the last to be recognized, but even this is not true. Note that the Muratorian canon most certainly did include Revelation.[252] What then of Hebrews?

One problem with identifying Hebrews' place in the canon is the confusion over the name given to it by the Church Fathers. Tertullian for example, lived at the same time as the Muratorian canon. In one of his works he refers to the "Scriptures" and then quotes "the epistle of Barnabas."[253] However, upon examining the quotation, it is not from the pseudepigraphal epistle of Barnabas at all, as some critics have argued, but it is a direct quote from

Hebrews 6:4-6.[254] In other words, the book of Hebrews was entitled "the epistle of Barnabas" owing to the western church's belief that Barnabas had written Hebrews. This is further supported by its appearance in the Codex Claremontanus by that same title.[255]

In addition Hebrews is quoted by many ante-Nicene Fathers as Scripture, long before Constantine's day. It is quoted as such by Justin Martyr, Irenaeus, Hippolytus, Clement of Alexandira, Cyril, Methodius, Tertullian, Origen, and Lactantius. It is also found in all the major Codices; the Sinaticus, Alexandrinus, Vaticanus, Ephraemi, and Claromontanus or Bezae. These are the oldest Codices known to exist. It is also found in the ancient *Didache*, or *Didascalia Apostolorum*, otherwise known as the "Teachings of the Apostles." Thus it seems obvious that by the end of the second century Hebrews was accepted as a part of canon, but there is good evidence that it was accepted long before then.

The disciples of the apostles are known the Apostolic Fathers. These were men who knew some of the apostles personally and had been taught by them, or by their disciples. The are the second and third generation of believers after the time of the apostles. Most of them lived from the middle of the first century into the early second. Unfortunately, most of their work has not survived the ages, but of those which have, Hebrews again finds a prominent place. Let us consider these writings.

Clement of Rome was taught by the apostle Paul himself (Philippians 4:3) and a prominent member of the early Roman church, having served as its bishop. In the chapter on Clement I already discussed his epistle and the fact that some even believe he was the author of Hebrews, but regardless of whether or not he wrote Hebrews, it is clear that Hebrews held a prominent place in Clement's writings just decades after its composition.

Second, the so-called Epistle of Barnabas dates to approximately 100 A.D.[256] It was written after the destruction of the Temple in 70 A.D. (to which it refers) and before the Bar Kochba revolt of 132 A.D. Although wrongly attributed to the Biblical Barnabas, it may have been authored by a Barnabas of Alexandria.[257] This confusion is ironically based, in part, upon the epistle's heavy use of the book of Hebrews.

Next we come to Ignatius who died around 111 A.D. Ignatius, though not mentioned in the Bible, was an acquaintance of Onesimus and allegedly tutored under the apostle John. Legend claims that he was the child called by Jesus in Matthew 18:2.[258] He became the bishop of Antioch, Syria[259] around 66 or 67 A.D. His surname, Theophorus means "the Bearer of God." He became a famous martyr under Trajan, where he was fed to wild beasts. Calmly entering the arena, Ignatius's words from his epistles were reflected in his death, as well as his life. "As the world hates the Christians, so God loves them."[260] In his surviving epistles he quotes from book of Hebrews.[261]

Thus we have three instances of epistles written at the end of the first century and/or the very beginning of the second, not more than three to four decades after Hebrews was written, which accept the epistles as a sacred text of Scripture. Critics have *no* evidence that anyone thought Hebrews to be a forgery of fake. They can only assume that its absence in some lists somehow demonstrates this belief. Nonetheless, the evidence is overwhelming that most ancients, dating back to the first century, accepted Hebrews as sacred canon. Who wrote the epistle was known to its reader, but it is not important to us. Nor is it important *per se* in determining what is canon.

Of the sixty-six books of the Bible, all the original recipients knew the author and accepted the writing, but if the book was not signed, and many were not, then the name of the author may have been lost to time and/or tradition. The sacred writing itself was never lost, nor questioned. Consider that of these sixty-six books we have only tradition to tell us the author of Genesis, Judges, Ruth, 1 & 2 Kings, 1 & 2 Chronicles, Esther, and Job. Should we really be so greatly concerned with who wrote Hebrews, when we realize that it *was* accepted by the apostolic fathers who tutored under the apostles?

It has been argued that the writings of the apostles were accepted from the very beginning as they were written.[262] This is partially true, but not entirely. It is possible that Paul wrote more letters than have become a part of the Bible, and it is certain that some writings of the apostles were debated for some time before becoming accepted. The early church was not naive and were cautious to insure that no false or heretical forgery made it into the canon. Because there were no church councils or popes to rule on these issues, there was occasional division as evidenced by the church father's writings. This, however, only further substantiates that the guiding force was the Holy Spirit, for it seems certain that at least twenty-five of the twenty-seven New Testament books were accepted as canon by the end of the second century, and probably much earlier. Hebrews was a part of that canon.

ENDNOTES

1 Eusebius, *Eusebius : The Church History* VI.25 Paul Meier, ed., Kregel Publications (Grand Rapids, Mich.) 1999 pg. 227
2 Warwick Aiken, Jr., "The Authorship of the Epistle to the Hebrew," *A Thesis for Dallas Theological Seminary* July 1946 pg. 51
3 Randall Price, *The Coming Last Days Temple* Harvest House (Eugene, OR) 1999 pg. 72
4 Note that I am neither a preterist nor partial preterist. I refer solely to the prophecy of Matthew 24:2 and Jewish history.
5 Robert Gundry, *A Survey of the New Testament* Zondervan (Grand Rapids, Mich.) 1994 pg. 424
6 Cf. R.C.H. Lenski, *The Interpretation of the Epistle to the Hebrews and of the Epistle of James* Lutheran Book Concern (Columbus, OH) 1938 pg. 10
7 Cf. for example, Josephus, "Antiquities of the Jews," XX.ix.1 *The Complete Works of Josephus* Kregel Publications (Grand Rapids, Mich.) 1981 pg. 423
8 David Criswell, *The Apostles After Jesus* Fortress Adonai (Dallas, TX) 2013 pg. 142
9 www.usatoday.com/story/money/business/2013/07/28/americans-poverty-no-work/2594203
10 David Allen, *Lukan Authorship of Hebrews* B&H Academic (Nashville, TN) 2010 pp. 90-91
11 Ibid.
12 Ibid. pg. 86
13 Ibid.
14 Ibid. pg. 87
15 Alexander Bruce, *The Epistle to the Hebrews* T&T Clark (Edinburgh, Scotland) 1899 pg. 21
16 Leon Morris, "Hebrews," *The Expositor's Bible Commentary* Vol. 12 Zondervan (Grand Rapids, Mich.) 1981 pg. 6
17 Alexander Nairne, *The Epistle to the Hebrews* Cambridge University Press (Cambridge, MS) 1917 pg. lvii
18 George Guthrie, "The Case for Apollos as the Author of Hebrews," *Faith and Mission* Vol. 18 No. 2 Spring 2001
19 Allen, *Lukan Authorship* op. cit. pg. 355
20 Ibid. pp. 360-362
21 Ibid.
22 Ibid.
23 Josephus, "Antiquities of the Jews," XX.ix.1 op. cit. pg. 423
24 Aiken, op. cit. pg. 34
25 Ibid.
26 Ibid. pg. 35
27 Ibid.
28 Henry Alford, *The Greek Testament* Rivington (London, England) 1875 pp. 64-65
29 F.W. Farrar, *The Epistle of Paul to the Hebrews* Cambridge Press (Cambridge, England) 1896 pg. 47
30 Aiken, op. cit. pg. 34

31 Josephus, "Antiquities of the Jews," XX.ix.1 op. cit. pg. 423
32 Theodore Zahn, *Introduction to the New Testament* T&T Clark (Edinburgh, Scotland) 1909 pg. 344
33 Cf. Ruth Hoppin, *Priscilla's Letter* Christian University Press (San Francisco, CA) 1997 pp. 125-175
34 Poeth, cited by Zahn, op. cit. pg. 338
35 Hoppin, *Priscilla's Letter* op. cit. pg. 126
36 Ibid.
37 Aiken, op. cit. pg. 30
38 Ibid. pg. 31
39 Ibid.
40 Samuel Davidson, *An Introduction to the Study of the New Testament* Longmans, Green, & Co. (London, England) 1882 pg. 266
41 Aiken, op. cit. pg. 31
42 See David Criswell, *The Apostles After Jesus* op. cit.
43 H. E. Dana & Julius Mantey, *A Manual Grammar of the Greek New Testament* MacMillan (New York, NY) 1940 pg. 81
44 Aiken, op. cit. pg. 38
45 Ibid. pg. 31
46 Richard Young, *Intermediate New Testament Greek* Broadman & Holman (Nashville, TN) 1994 pg. 8
47 A. T. Robertson, *A Grammar of the Greek New Testament in Light of Historical Research* Harper & Row (New York, NY) 1931 pg. 578
48 Alford, op. cit. pg. 68
49 Allen, *Lukan Authorship* op. cit. pg. 352
50 Severian of Galba, *Ancient Christian Commentary on Scripture Vol. X* Erik Heen, Philip Krey, eds. Intervarsity Press (Downers Grove, Ill.) 2005 pg. 2
51 Allen, *Lukan Authorship* op. cit. pg. 27
52 http://cjlit.blogspot.com/2007/07/book-of-hebrews-and-clement-of-rome.html
53 William Barclay, *The Letter to the Hebrews* Westminister John Knox Press (Lousville, NY) 1955 pg. 2
54 Farrar, op. cit. pg. 47
55 Ibid. pg. 43
56 Eusebius, *The Church History* VI.14 op. cit. pg. 217
57 Barnes, *Notes - One Volume ed.* op. cit. pg. 1215
58 Aiken, op. cit. pg. 20
59 F.F. Bruce, *The Epistle to the Hebrews* Wm. B. Eerdmans (Grand Rapids, Mich.) 1964 pg. xxxvi
60 Brooke Westcott, *The Epistle to the Hebrews* Wm. B. Eerdmans (Grand Rapids, Mich.) 1970 pg. lxii
61 Bruce, op. cit. pg. xxxviii
62 Severian of Gabala, *Ancient Christian Commentary on Scripture Vol. X* op. cit. pg. 2
63 Ibid.
64 R.C.H. Lenski, *The Interpretation of the Epistle to the Hebrews and of the Epistle of James* Lutheran Book Concern (Columbus, OH) 1938 pg. 9
65 Theodore of Mapsustia, *Ancient Christian Commentary on Scripture Vol. X* op. cit. pg. 1

66 Thomas Aquinas, *Commentary on the Epistle to the Hebrews* St. Augustine Press (South Bend, IN) 2006 pg. 7
67 Ibid.
68 J. Dwight Pentecost, *A Faith That Endures* Discovery House (Grand Rapids, Mich.) 1992 pg. 9
69 Aquinas, op. cit. pg. 7
70 Merrill Unger, *Unger's Bible Dictionary* Moody Press (Chicago, Ill.) 1957 pg. 465
71 H.A. Ironside, *Studies in the Epistle to the Hebrews* Loizeaux Brothers (New York, NY) 1932 pg. 135
72 Severian of Gabala, *Ancient Christian Commentary on Scripture Vol. X* op. cit. pg. 2
73 Robert Govett, *Govett on Hebrews* Conley & Schuesttle (Miami Springs, FL) 1981 pg. 1
74 Lenski, op. cit. pg. 9
75 Allen, *Lukan Authorship* op. cit. pg. 27
76 Aiken, op. cit. pg. 72
77 By this I mean that those of us who believe in the unerring Word of God, free translation are problematic because they often reinterpret the words of the author rather than allowing those words to speak for themselves. A literal translation is best for it seeks to remain as close to the original text as possible.
78 James Dunn, cited by David Wenham, "Unity and Diversity in the New Testament," *A Theology of the New Testament by George Eldon Ladd* Wm. B. Eerdmans (Grand Rapids, Mich.) 1974 pg. 686
79 Wenham, op. cit. pg. 685
80 Ibid. pg. 704
81 Aiken, op. cit. pg. 53
82 Charles Erdman, *The Epistle to the Hebrews* Westminister (Philadelphia, PN) 1934 pp. 12-13
83 John Ebrard, *A Biblical Commentary on the Epistle to the Hebrews* T&T Clark (Edinburgh, Scotland) 1853 pg. 408
84 Aiken, op. cit. pg. 45
85 Ibid. pg. 67
86 Bruce Metzger, *A Textual Commentary on the Greek New Testament* United Bible Societies (Stuttgart, Germany) 1994 pg. 601
87   Zane Hodges "Hebrews," *The Bible Knowledge Commentary : New Testament* John Walvoord & Roy Zuck, eds., Victor Books (Wheaton, Ill.) 1986 pg. 777
88   Dionysius of Corinth, "Letter to the Roman Church," III, *Ante-Nicene Fathers Vol. 8* Alexander Roberts & James Donaldson, eds., Charles Scribner (New York, NY) 1886 pg. 765
89 John Foxe, *Acts and Monuments of the Church   Vol. 1* Religious Tract Society (London, England) 1853 reprint pg. 104
90 *Pseudo-Abdias*, as cited by Foxe, op. cit. pg. 103
91 Foxe, op. cit. pg. 104
92 H.A. Ironside, *Studies in the Epistle to the Heberws and Epistle to Titus* Loizeaux Brothers (Neptune, NJ) 1932 pg. 10
93 Robert Gromacki, *Stand Bold in Grace* Baker Books (Grand Rapids, Mich.) 1984 pg. 12

94 Aiken, op. cit. pg. 49
95 http://articles.ochristian.com/article15617.shtml
96 Erdman, op. cit. pg. 13
97 James Moffatt *A Critical and Exegetical Commentary on the Epistle to the Hebrews* Charles Scribners (New York, NY) 1924 pg. xviii (Cf. Tertullian, "On Modesty" xx *Ante-Nicene Fathers Vol. 4* Alexander Roberts & James Donaldson, eds., Charles Scribner (New York, NY) 1886 pg. 97)
98 Hodges, op. cit. pg. 778
99 Ibid.
100 Cleveland Coxe, "The Epistle of Barnabas," *Ante-Nicene Fathers Vol. 1* Alexander Roberts & James Donaldson, eds., Charles Scribner (New York, NY) 1885 pg. 133
101 http://www.newadvent.org/cathen/01637a.htm
102 See notes on Mark and Barnabas in Criswell, *Apostles After Jesus* op. cit.
103 Ibid.
104 Coxe, *Ante-Nicene Fathers Vol. 1* op. cit. pg. 133
105 Ironside, op. cit. pg. 8
106 Hoppin, *Priscilla's Letter* op. cit. pg. 61
107 Cf. Bernhard Weiss, *A Manual of Introduction to the New Testament* Funk & Wagnalls (New York, NY) 1889 pg. 15
108 Lenski, op. cit. pg. 11
109 John Owens, *Exposition of the Epistle to the Hebrews Vol. 1* Johnstone & Hunter (Edinburgh, Scotland) 1854 pg. 70
110 "Regonitions of Clement," *Ante-Nicene Fathers Vol. 7* Alexander Roberts & James Donaldson, eds., Charles Scribner (New York, NY) 1886 pp. 78-80
111 Criswell, *Apostles After Jesus* op. cit. pg. 163
112 Ibid. pg. 164
113 Thieleman J. van Braght, *Martyrs' Mirror* Herald Press (Scottdale, PN) 1950 ed. (1660 orig.) pg. 76
114 John Foxe, *Foxe's Book of Martyrs* Clarion Classics (Grand Rapids, Mich.) 1926 (abridged ed.) pg. 5
115 Criswell, *Apostles After Jesus* op. cit. pg. 164
116 Hodges op. cit. pg. 778
117 Govett, op. cit. pg. 1
118 Aiken, op. cit. pg. 72
119 F.F. Bruce, *The Epistle to the Hebrews* Wm. B. Eerdmans (Grand Rapids, Mich.) 1964 pg. xxxix
120 Ibid.
121 Lenski, op. cit. pg. 9
122 Aiken, op. cit. pg. 72
123 Ibid.
124 Allen, *Lukan Authorship* op. cit. pg. 27
125 Ibid. pg. 86
126 Ibid.
127 Ibid. pg. 87
128 Aiken, op. cit. pg. 79
129 Allen, *Lukan Authorship* op. cit. pp. 196-260
130 http://www.levitt.com/essays/luke
131 Ibid.

132 http://www.rwaynestacy.com/2011/03/was-luke-gentile.html
133 http://www.levitt.com/essays/luke
134 Ibid.
135 Ibid.
136 Ibid.
137 Allen, *Lukan Authorship* op. cit. pg. 266
138 George Milligan, *The New Testament Documents: Their Origin and Early History*, Macmillan and Co. (London, England) 1913 pg. 149
139 Franz Delitzsch, *A Commentary on the Epistle to the Hebrews* T&T Clark (Edinburgh, Scotland) 1868 pg. 415
140 Ibid.
141 Ibid.
142 Ibid.
143 Martin Luther, *Erlangen* ed. 18, 38 as cited by R.C.H. Lenski, *The Interpretation of the Epistle to the Hebrews and of the Epistle of James* Lutheran Book Concern (Columbus, OH) 1938 pg. 21
144 http://judaismvschristianity.com/hebrews.htm
145 Ibid.
146 Ironside, op. cit. pg. 8
147 Aiken, op. cit. pg. 82
148 Farrar, op. cit. pg. 332
149 Paul Ellington, *Epistle in Hebrews* Eerdmans (Grand Rapids, Mich.) 1993 pg. 21
150 Lesly Massey, *Women in the Church* McFarland (Jefferson, NC) 2002 pg. 23
151 Ruth Hoppin, *Priscilla, Author of the Epistle to the Hebrews* Exposition Press (New York, NY) 1969 pg. 20
152 Hoppin, *Priscilla's Letter* op. cit. pg. 23
153 Hoppin, *Priscilla, Author of the Epistle to the Hebrews* op. cit. pg. 22
154 http://polumeros.blogspot.com/2009/01/is-priscilla-author-of-hebrews.html
155 Hoppin, *Priscilla's Letter* op. cit. pp. 23-32
156 Ibid. pp. 16-19
157 Hoppin, *Priscilla, Author of the Epistle to the Hebrews* op. cit. pg. 32
158 Hoppin, *Priscilla's Letter* op. cit. pg. 50
159 Ibid. pg. 4
160 Hoppin, *Priscilla, Author of the Epistle to the Hebrews* op. cit. pg. 18
161 Hoppin, *Priscilla's Letter* op. cit. pp. 12-14
162 Ibid. pg. 81
163 Ibid.
164 Ibid.
165 Ibid. pg. 86
166 C. Bernard Ruffin, *The Twelve* Our Sunday Visitor (Huntington, In.) 1997 pp. 50-51
167 Criswell, *The Apostles After Jesus* op. cit. pg. 75
168 Ibid. pg. 27
169 Hoppin, *Priscilla's Letter* op. cit. pp. 125-175
170 Criswell, *The Apostles After Jesus* op. cit. pg. 162
171 Ibid.
172 Ibid. pg. 172

173 Ibid. pp. 162-182

174 www.tertullian.org/fathers/chronography_of_354_13_bishops_of_rome.htm

175 J.N.D. Kelly, *The Oxford Dicationary of Popes* Oxford Press (Oxford, England) 1986 pp. 7-8

176 www.scrollpublishing.com/store/Clement-of-Rome.html

177 The antiquity of the tradition also supports the early date, whereas later revisions were probably made to accomodate the alleged papacy of Peter.

178 Edgar Goodspeed, "First Clement Called Forth by Hebrews," *Journal of Biblical Literature Vol. 30 No. 2* 1911 pg. 157

179 Erdman, op. cit. pg. 13

180 Eusebius, *Church History* VI.25 op. cit. pg. 227

181 Bruce, *The Epistle to the Hebrews* op. cit. pg. xxxix

182 Aiken, op. cit. pg. 46

183 Lenski, op. cit. pg. 9

184 Benjamin Bacon, "The Doctrine of Faith in Hebrews, James, and Clement of Rome,"*Journal of Biblical Literature Vol. 19 No. 1* 1900 pg. 19

185 Ibid. pg. 15

186 Ibid. pg. 18

187 Edgar Goodspeed, "First Clement Called Forth by Hebrews," *Journal of Biblical Literature Vol. 30 No. 2* 1911 pg. 159

188 Owens, op. cit. pg. 72

189 Philip Schaff, *History of the Christian Church Vol. 2* Hendrickson Publishers (Peabody, Mass.) 1996 pg. 158

190 www.newadvent.org/cathen/04012c.htm

191 www.religionfacts.com/christianity/people/clement_rome.htm

192 www.scrollpublishing.com/store/Clement-of-Rome.html

193 J.B. Lightfoot & J.R. Hammer, eds., *The Apostolic Fathers* Baker Book House (Grand Rapids, Mich.) 1984 pg. 3

194 David Criswell, *Controversies in the Gospels* Fortress Adonai (Dallas, TX) 2012 pg. 393

195 Criswell, *Apostles of Jesus* op. cit. pg. 179

196 Steven Ger, *The Book of Hebrews : Christ is Greater* AMG (Chattanooga, TN) 2009 pg. 6

197 Aiken, op. cit. pg. 10

198 Braght, op. cit. pg. 86

199 Criswell, *Apostles of Jesus* op. cit. pp. 169-173

200 Ibid.

201 Eusebius, 4.11 op. cit. pg. 143

202 Criswell, *Apostles of Jesus* op. cit. pp. 169-173

203 Aiken, op. cit. pg. 9

204 Criswell, *Controversies in the Gospels* op. cit. pp. 209-210

205 Ebrard, op. cit. pg. 422

206 Lenski, op. cit. pg. 13

207 Owens, op. cit. pg. 72

208 Tertullian, "On Modesty" xx *Ante-Nicene Fathers Vol. 4* Alexander Roberts & James Donaldson, eds., Charles Scribner (New York, NY) 1886 pg. 97

209 Cited in Steven Ger, *The Book of Hebrews : Christ is Greater* AMG (Chattanooga, TN) 2009 pg. 7

210 Erdman, op. cit. pg. 13
211 Papias, "Fragments from Papias," v. *Apostolic Fathers* op. cit. pg. 530
212 Also see Eusebius, 3.39 *Church History* op. cit. pg. 127
213 Moffatt, op. cit. pg. xx
214 www.catholic.org/saints/saint.php?saint_id=1543
215 http://oca.org/saints/lives/2013/09/03/102483-martyr-aristion-the-bishop-of-alexandria
216 Cf. Hoppin, *Priscilla's Letter* op. cit. pg. 74
217 Van Braght, op. cit. pg. 86
218 Ibid.
219 George Guthrie *NIV Application Commentary : Hebrews* Zondervan (Grand Rapids, Mich.) 1998 pg. 23
220 Ger, op. cit. pg. 6
221 Ibid.
222 Unger, op. cit. pp. 552-553
223 Ruffin, op. cit. pg. 80
224 Cf. John Gill, "Commentary on the New Testament," John 19:25 E-Sword Software Commentary Series
225 Ibid.
226 Ibid.
227 If the reader is not convinced yet, then I refer him to my other books, *Controversies in the Acts and Epistles* and *Apostles After Christ* where I discuss this topin more depth.
228 Eusebius, 4.5, op. cit. pg. 137
229 Eusebius places thirteen bishops in a very short time, and places Jude last when he would have been extremely old. See *The Apostles After Jesus* for more in this.
230 Hippolytus, "On the Twelve Apostles," *Ante-Nicene Fathers Vol. 8* op. cit. pp. 254-256
231 Charles Erdman, *The Epistle to the Hebrews* Westminister (Philadelphia, PN) 1934 pg. 13
232 Cf. Cornelius Stam, *The Epistle to the Hebrews – Who Wrote it and Why?* Beream Bible (Germantown, WI) 1991 pg. 15
233 Ger, op. cit. pg. 5
234 Criswell, *The Apostles After Jesus* op. cit. pp. 30-34
235 Erdman, op. cit. pg. 13
236 Ruffin, op. cit. pp. 104-105
237 Clement of Alexandria, "Miscellanies," 3.6.52 *Ante-Nicene Fathers Vol. 2* Alexander Roberts & James Donaldson, eds., Charles Scribner (New York, NY) 1886 pg. 390
238 Polycrates, quoted by Eusebius, *The Church History*, 3.31 op. cit. pg. 119
239 Criswell, *The Apostles After Jesus* op. cit. pp. 63-64
240 Ibid. pg. 178
241 Barclay Newman, ed., *A Concise Greek-English Dictionary* United Bible Society (Stuttgart, Germany) 1971 pg. 41
242 Metzger, *A Textual Commentary* op. cit. pg. 607
243 paulandco-workers.blogspot.com/2010/08/titus-timothy-passed-as-jew.html
244 Farrar, op. cit. pg. 48

245 This is not an exact quote, but it is the standard logic pattern for deduction expressed in Holmes novels. Cf. Sir Arthur Conan Doyle, "A Study in Scarlet," *The Complete Works of Sherlock Holmes* Barnes & Noble Books (New York, NY) 1992 ed. D pp. 21-25
246 Eusebius, *Church History* VI.25 op. cit. pg. 227
247 Randall Price, *Searching for the Original Bible* Harvest House (Eugene, OR) 2007 pg. 156
248 Cf. Lee Martin McDonald, *The Biblical Canon* Hendrickson Publishers (Peabody, Mass.) 1995
249 Brian Edwards, *Nothing but the Truth* Evangelical Press (Webster, NY) 2006 ed. pg. 218
250 http://www.christian-history.org/muratorian-canon.html
251 Edwards, op. cit. pg. 218
252 http://www.christian-history.org/muratorian-canon.html
253 Tertullian, "On Modesty" xx *Ante-Nicene Fathers Vol. 4* Alexander Roberts & James Donaldson, eds., Charles Scribner (New York, NY) 1886 pg. 97
254 Ibid.
255 Hodges, op. cit. pg. 778
256 Cleveland Coxe, "The Epistle of Barnabas," *Ante-Nicene Fathers Vol. 1* Alexander Roberts & James Donaldson, eds., Charles Scribner (New York, NY) 1885 pg. 133
257 http://www.newadvent.org/cathen/01637a.htm
258 Coxe, *Ante-Nicene Fathers Vol. 1* op. cit. pg. 45
259 Eusebius, 3.36 op. cit. pg. 123
260 Ibid.
261 Ignatius, "To the Trallians," II, IX, *Ante-Nicene Fathers Vol. 1* op. cit. pp. 66, 70
262 Edwards, op. cit. pg. 226

WORKS CITED

Books

Henry Alford, *The Greek Testament* Rivington (London, England) 1875

David Allen, *Lukan Authorship of Hebrews* B&H Academic (Nashville, TN) 2010

Thomas Aquinas, *Commentary on the Epistle to the Hebrews* St. Augustine Press (South Bend, IN) 2006

William Barclay, *The Letter to the Hebrews* Westminister John Knox Press (Lousville, NY) 1955

Thieleman J. van Braght, *Martyrs' Mirror* Herald Press (Scottdale, PN) 1950 ed. (1660 orig.)

Alexander Bruce, *The Epistle to the Hebrews* T&T Clark (Edinburgh, Scotland) 1899

F.F. Bruce, *The Epistle to the Hebrews* Wm. B. Eerdmans (Grand Rapids, Mich.) 1964

David Criswell, *The Apostles After Jesus* Fortress Adonai (Dallas, TX) 2013

David Criswell, *Controversies in the Gospels* Fortress Adonai (Dallas, TX) 2012

H. E. Dana & Julius Mantey, *A Manual Grammar of the Greek New Testament* MacMillan (New York, NY) 1940

Samuel Davidson, *An Introduction to the Study of the New Testament* Longmans, Green, & Co. (London, England) 1882

Franz Delitzsch, *A Commentary on the Epistle to the Hebrews* T&T Clark (Edinburgh, Scotland) 1868

Sir Arthur Conan Doyle, *The Complete Works of Sherlock Holmes* Barnes & Noble Books (New York, NY) 1992

John Ebrard, *A Biblical Commentary on the Epistle to the Hebrews* T&T Clark (Edinburgh, Scotland) 1853

Brian Edwards, *Nothing but the Truth* Evangelical Press (Webster, NY) 2006

Paul Ellington, *Epistle in Hebrews* Eerdmans (Grand Rapids, Mich.) 1993

Charles Erdman, *The Epistle to the Hebrews* Westminister (Philadelphia, PN) 1934

Eusebius, *Eusebius : The Church History* VI.25 Paul Meier, ed., Kregel Publications (Grand Rapids, Mich.) 1999

F.W. Farrar, *The Epistle of Paul to the Hebrews* Cambridge Press (Cambridge, England) 1896

John Foxe, *Acts and Monuments of the Church Vol. 1* Religious Tract Society (London, England) 1853

John Foxe, *Foxe's Book of Martyrs* Clarion Classics (Grand Rapids, Mich.) 1926 (abridged ed.)

Steven Ger, *The Book of Hebrews : Christ is Greater* AMG (Chattanooga, TN) 2009

Robert Govett, *Govett on Hebrews* Conley & Schuesttle (Miami Springs, FL) 1981

Robert Gromacki, *Stand Bold in Grace* Baker Books (Grand Rapids, Mich.) 1984

Robert Gundry, *A Survey of the New Testament* Zondervan (Grand Rapids, Mich.) 1994 pg. 424

George Guthrie *NIV Application Commentary : Hebrews* Zondervan (Grand Rapids, Mich.) 1998

Ruth Hoppin, *Priscilla, Author of the Epistle to the Hebrews* Exposition Press (New York, NY) 1969

Ruth Hoppin, *Priscilla's Letter* Christian University Press (San Francisco, CA) 1997

H.A. Ironside, *Studies in the Epistle to the Hebrews* Loizeaux Brothers (New York, NY) 1932

H.A. Ironside, *Studies in the Epistle to the Hebrews and Epistle to Titus* Loizeaux Brothers (Neptune, NJ) 1932

Josephus, *The Complete Works of Josephus* Kregel Publications (Grand Rapids, Mich.) 1981

J.N.D. Kelly, *The Oxford Dicationary of Popes* Oxford Press (Oxford, England) 1986

George Eldon Ladd, *A Theology of the New Testament by George Eldon Ladd* Wm. B. Eerdmans (Grand Rapids, Mich.) 1974

R.C.H. Lenski, *The Interpretation of the Epistle to the Hebrews and of the Epistle of James* Lutheran Book Concern (Columbus, OH) 1938

J.B. Lightfoot & J.R. Hammer, eds., *The Apostolic Fathers* Baker Book House (Grand Rapids, Mich.) 1984

Lee Martin McDonald, *The Biblical Canon* Hendrickson Publishers (Peabody, Mass.) 1995

Lesly Massey, *Women in the Church* McFarland (Jefferson, NC) 2002

Bruce Metzger, *A Textual Commentary on the Greek New Testament* United Bible Societies (Stuttgart, Germany) 1994

George Milligan, *The New Testament Documents: Their Origin and Early History*, Macmillan and Co. (London, England) 1913

James Moffatt *A Critical and Exegetical Commentary on the Epistle to the Hebrews* Charles Scribners (New York, NY) 1924

Alexander Nairne, *The Epistle to the Hebrews* Cambridge University Press (Cambridge, MS) 1917

John Owens, *Exposition of the Epistle to the Hebrews Vol. 1* Johnstone & Hunter (Edinburgh, Scotland) 1854

J. Dwight Pentecost, *A Faith That Endures* Discovery House (Grand Rapids, Mich.) 1992

Randall Price, *The Coming Last Days Temple* Harvest House (Eugene, OR) 1999 pg. 72

Randall Price, *Searching for the Original Bible* Harvest House (Eugene, OR) 2007

A. T. Robertson, *A Grammar of the Greek New Testament in Light of Historical Research* Harper & Row (New York, NY) 1931

C. Bernard Ruffin, *The Twelve* Our Sunday Visitor (Huntington, In.) 1997

Philip Schaff, *History of the Christian Church Vol. 2* Hendrickson Publishers (Peabody, Mass.) 1996

Cornelius Stam, *The Epistle to the Hebrews – Who Wrote it and Why?* Beream Bible (Germantown, WI) 1991

Merrill Unger, *Unger's Bible Dictionary* Moody Press (Chicago, Ill.) 1957

Thieleman J. van Braght, *Martyrs' Mirror* Herald Press (Scottdale, PN) 1950 ed. (1660 orig.)

Bernhard Weiss, *A Manual of Introduction to the New Testament* Funk & Wagnalls (New York, NY) 1889

Brooke Westcott, *The Epistle to the Hebrews* Wm. B. Eerdmans (Grand Rapids, Mich.) 1970

Richard Young, *Intermediate New Testament Greek* Broadman & Holman (Nashville, TN) 1994

Theodore Zahn, *Introduction to the New Testament* T&T Clark (Edinburgh, Scotland) 1909

Periodicals
Benjamin Bacon, "The Doctrine of Faith in Hebrews, James, and Clement of Rome," *Journal of Biblical Literature* Vol. 19 No. 1 1900

Edgar Goodspeed, "First Clement Called Forth by Hebrews," *Journal of Biblical Literature* Vol. 30 No. 2 1911

George Guthrie, "The Case for Apollos as the Author of Hebrews," *Faith and Mission* Vol. 18 No. 2 Spring 2001

Reference Works
Frank Gaebelain, ed., *The Expositor's Bible Commentary Vol. 12* Zondervan (Grand Rapids, Mich.) 1981

Erik Heen, Philip Krey, eds. *Ancient Christian Commentary on Scripture Vol. X* Intervarsity Press (Downers Grove, Ill.) 2005

Barclay Newman, ed., *A Concise Greek-English Dictionary* United Bible Society (Stuttgart, Germany) 1971

Alexander Roberts & James Donaldson, eds., *Ante-Nicene Fathers Vol. 1* Charles Scribner (New York, NY) 1885

Alexander Roberts & James Donaldson, eds., *Ante-Nicene Fathers Vol. 2* Charles Scribner (New York, NY) 1886

Alexander Roberts & James Donaldson, eds., *Ante-Nicene Fathers Vol. 4* Charles Scribner (New York, NY) 1886

Alexander Roberts & James Donaldson, eds., *Ante-Nicene Fathers Vol. 7* Charles Scribner (New York, NY) 1886

Alexander Roberts & James Donaldson, eds., *Ante-Nicene Fathers Vol. 8* Charles Scribner (New York, NY) 1886

John Walvoord & Roy Zuck, eds., *The Bible Knowledge Commentary : New Testament* Victor Books (Wheaton, Ill.) 1986

Miscelaneous
Warwick Aiken, Jr., "The Authorship of the Epistle to the Hebrew," *A Thesis for Dallas Theological Seminary* July 1946

John Gill, "Commentary on the New Testament," E-Sword Software Commentary Series

articles.ochristian.com/article15617.shtml

cjlit.blogspot.com/2007/07/book-of-hebrews-and-clement-of-rome.html

judaismvschristianity.com/hebrews.htm

oca.org/saints/lives/2013/09/03/102483-martyr-aristion-the-bishop-of-alexandria

paulandco-workers.blogspot.com/2010/08/titus-timothy-passed-as-jew.html

polumeros.blogspot.com/2009/01/is-priscilla-author-of-hebrews.html

www.catholic.org/saints/saint.php?saint_id=1543

www.christian-history.org/muratorian-canon.html

www.levitt.com/essays/luke

www.newadvent.org/cathen/01637a.htm

www.newadvent.org/cathen/04012c.htm

www.religionfacts.com/christianity/people/clement_rome.htm

www.rwaynestacy.com/2011/03/was-luke-gentile.html

www.scrollpublishing.com/store/Clement-of-Rome.html

www.tertullian.org/fathers/chronography_of_354_13_bishops_of_rome.htm

www.usatoday.com/story/money/business/2013/07/28/americans-poverty-no-work/2594203

ingramcontent.com/pod-product-compliance
ng Source LLC
rsburg PA
71506040426
B00008B/1516